TRADE ISSUES, POLICIES AND LAWS

NAFTA AT 20

OVERVIEW, TRADE EFFECTS, AND IMPACT ON AGRICULTURE

TRADE ISSUES, POLICIES AND LAWS

TRADE ISSUES, POLICIES AND LAWS

NAFTA AT 20

OVERVIEW, TRADE EFFECTS, AND IMPACT ON AGRICULTURE

MARIAN WEAVER
EDITOR

nova publishers
New York

Library of Congress Cataloging-in-Publication Data

ISBN: 978-1-63482-779-9

Published by Nova Science Publishers, Inc. † New York

CONTENTS

PREFACE

This book provides an overview of North American trade liberalization before NAFTA, an overview of NAFTA provisions, the economic effects of NAFTA, and policy considerations. This book also examines the integration of North America's agricultural and food markets as a result of the North American Free Trade Agreement.

Chapter 1 – The North American Free Trade Agreement (NAFTA) entered into force on January 1, 1994. The agreement was signed by President George H.W. Bush on December 17, 1992, and approved by Congress on November 20, 1993. The NAFTA Implementation Act was signed into law by President William J. Clinton on December 8, 1993 (P.L. 103-182). The overall economic impact of NAFTA is difficult to measure since trade and investment trends are influenced by numerous other economic variables, such as economic growth, inflation, and currency fluctuations. The agreement may have accelerated the trade liberalization that was already taking place, but many of these changes may have taken place with or without an agreement. Nevertheless, NAFTA is significant because it was the most comprehensive free trade agreement (FTA) negotiated at the time and contained several groundbreaking provisions. A legacy of the agreement is that it has served as a template or model for the new generation of FTAs that the United States later negotiated and it also served as a template for certain provisions in multilateral trade negotiations as part of the Uruguay Round.

The 113th Congress faces numerous issues related to international trade. Canada and Mexico are the first and third largest U.S. trading partners, respectively. With the two countries participating in the negotiations to conclude a Trans-Pacific Partnership (TPP) free trade agreement among the United States and 11 other countries, policy issues related to NAFTA continue to be of interest for Congress. If an agreement is concluded, it could affect the rules and market access commitments governing North American trade and investment since NAFTA entered into force. A related trade policy issue in which the effects of NAFTA may be explored is the possible renewal of Trade Promotion Authority (TPA; formerly known as "fast-track authority") to provide expedited procedures for the consideration of bills to implement trade agreements.

NAFTA was controversial when first proposed, mostly because it was the first FTA involving two wealthy, developed countries and a developing country. The political debate surrounding the agreement was divisive with proponents arguing that the agreement would help generate thousands of jobs and reduce income disparity in the region, while opponents warned that the agreement would cause huge job losses in the United States as companies moved production to Mexico to lower costs. In reality, NAFTA did not cause the huge job losses feared by the critics or the large economic gains predicted by supporters. The net overall effect of NAFTA on the U.S. economy appears to have been relatively modest, primarily because trade with Canada and Mexico account for a small percentage of U.S. GDP. However, there were worker and firm adjustment costs as the three countries adjusted to more open trade and investment among their economies.

The rising number of bilateral and regional trade agreements throughout the world and the rising presence of China in Latin America could have implications for U.S. trade policy with its NAFTA partners. Some proponents of open and rules-based trade maintain that a further deepening of economic relations with Canada and Mexico will help promote a common trade agenda with shared values and generate economic growth. Some opponents argue that the agreement has caused worker displacement and that NAFTA needs to be reopened. One possible way of doing this is through the proposed TPP. The ongoing TPP negotiations, launched in the fall of 2008, may not result in a reopening of NAFTA, but could alter some of the rules and market access commitments governing North American trade and investment.

Chapter 2 - This report examines the integration of North America's agricultural and food markets as a result of the North American Free Trade Agreement (NAFTA), implemented in 1994. NAFTA has had a profound effect on many aspects of North American agriculture over the past two decades. With a few exceptions, intraregional agricultural trade is now completely free of tariff and quota restrictions, and the agricultural sectors of the member countries—Canada, Mexico, and the United States—have become far more integrated, as is evidenced by rising trade in a wider range of agricultural products, substantial levels of cross-border investment, and important changes in consumption and production. The report also examines recent disputes among its constituents and identifies opportunities for further reforms of mutual benefit to the member countries, with particular attention devoted to the NAFTA governments' efforts to seek deeper regional integration through such means as regulatory cooperation and modifying the agreement's rules of origin and broader access to markets in other parts of the world through the negotiation of additional free-trade agreements.

In: NAFTA at 20
Editor: Marian Weaver
ISBN: 978-1-63482-779-9

Chapter 1

NAFTA AT 20: OVERVIEW AND TRADE EFFECTS*

M. Angeles Villarreal and Ian F. Fergusson

SUMMARY

The North American Free Trade Agreement (NAFTA) entered into force on January 1, 1994. The agreement was signed by President George H.W. Bush on December 17, 1992, and approved by Congress on November 20, 1993. The NAFTA Implementation Act was signed into law by President William J. Clinton on December 8, 1993 (P.L. 103-182). The overall economic impact of NAFTA is difficult to measure since trade and investment trends are influenced by numerous other economic variables, such as economic growth, inflation, and currency fluctuations. The agreement may have accelerated the trade liberalization that was already taking place, but many of these changes may have taken place with or without an agreement. Nevertheless, NAFTA is significant because it was the most comprehensive free trade agreement (FTA) negotiated at the time and contained several groundbreaking provisions. A legacy of the agreement is that it has served as a template or model for the new generation of FTAs that the United States later negotiated and it also served as a template for certain provisions in multilateral trade negotiations as part of the Uruguay Round.

* This is an edited, reformatted and augmented version of a Congressional Research Service publication R42965, prepared for Members and Committees of Congress dated April 28, 2014.

The 113th Congress faces numerous issues related to international trade. Canada and Mexico are the first and third largest U.S. trading partners, respectively. With the two countries participating in the negotiations to conclude a Trans-Pacific Partnership (TPP) free trade agreement among the United States and 11 other countries, policy issues related to NAFTA continue to be of interest for Congress. If an agreement is concluded, it could affect the rules and market access commitments governing North American trade and investment since NAFTA entered into force. A related trade policy issue in which the effects of NAFTA may be explored is the possible renewal of Trade Promotion Authority (TPA; formerly known as "fast-track authority") to provide expedited procedures for the consideration of bills to implement trade agreements.

NAFTA was controversial when first proposed, mostly because it was the first FTA involving two wealthy, developed countries and a developing country. The political debate surrounding the agreement was divisive with proponents arguing that the agreement would help generate thousands of jobs and reduce income disparity in the region, while opponents warned that the agreement would cause huge job losses in the United States as companies moved production to Mexico to lower costs. In reality, NAFTA did not cause the huge job losses feared by the critics or the large economic gains predicted by supporters. The net overall effect of NAFTA on the U.S. economy appears to have been relatively modest, primarily because trade with Canada and Mexico account for a small percentage of U.S. GDP. However, there were worker and firm adjustment costs as the three countries adjusted to more open trade and investment among their economies.

The rising number of bilateral and regional trade agreements throughout the world and the rising presence of China in Latin America could have implications for U.S. trade policy with its NAFTA partners. Some proponents of open and rules-based trade maintain that a further deepening of economic relations with Canada and Mexico will help promote a common trade agenda with shared values and generate economic growth. Some opponents argue that the agreement has caused worker displacement and that NAFTA needs to be reopened. One possible way of doing this is through the proposed TPP. The ongoing TPP negotiations, launched in the fall of 2008, may not result in a reopening of NAFTA, but could alter some of the rules and market access commitments governing North American trade and investment.

INTRODUCTION

The North American Free Trade Agreement (NAFTA) has been in effect since January 1, 1994. Signed by President George H.W. Bush on December 17, 1992, and approved by Congress on November 20, 1993, the NAFTA Implementation Act was signed into law by President William J. Clinton on December 8, 1993 (P.L. 103-182). NAFTA continues to be of interest to Congress because of the importance of Canada and Mexico as U.S. trading partners, and also because of the implications NAFTA has for U.S. trade policy. This report provides an overview of North American trade liberalization before NAFTA, an overview of NAFTA provisions, the economic effects of NAFTA, and policy considerations.

The 113th Congress, in both its legislative and oversight capacities, faces numerous issues related to international trade. The Obama Administration has made the proposed Trans-Pacific Partnership (TPP) free trade agreement one of its top trade priorities.[1] The United States, Canada, and Mexico, along with nine other countries, are participating in the TPP negotiations. If negotiations continue to move forward, it may affect the rules and market access commitments governing North American trade since NAFTA entered into force. A related trade policy issue in which the effects of NAFTA may be explored is the possible renewal of Trade Promotion Authority (TPA; formerly known as "fast-track authority") to provide expedited procedures for the consideration of bills to implement trade agreements.[2]

Many trade policy experts give credit to free trade agreements (FTAs) for enhancing economic linkages between countries, creating more efficient production processes, increasing the availability of lower-priced consumer goods, and improving living standards and working conditions.[3] Others have blamed FTAs for disappointing employment trends and for not having done enough to improve competitiveness, labor standards, and environmental conditions abroad.[4]

A legacy of NAFTA is that it has served as a model for other FTAs that the United States later negotiated and also for multilateral negotiations. NAFTA initiated a new generation of trade agreements in the Western Hemisphere and other parts of the world, influencing negotiations in areas such as market access, rules of origin, intellectual property rights, foreign investment, dispute resolution, worker rights, and environmental protection. The United States currently has FTAs with 20 countries. As with NAFTA, these trade agreements have often been supported or criticized on similar arguments related to jobs.

MARKET OPENING PRIOR TO NAFTA

The concept of economic integration in North America was not a new one at the time NAFTA negotiations started. In 1911, President William Howard Taft signed a reciprocal trade agreement with Canadian Prime Minister Sir Wilfred Laurier. After a bitter election, Canadians rejected free trade and ousted Prime Minister Laurier, thereby ending the agreement. In 1965, the United States and Canada signed the U.S.-Canada Automotive Products Agreement that liberalized trade in cars, trucks, tires, and automotive parts between the two countries.[5] The Auto Pact was credited as a pioneer in creating an integrated North American automotive sector. In the case of Mexico, the government had been implementing reform measures since the mid-1980s, prior to NAFTA, to liberalize its economy. By 1990, when NAFTA negotiations began, Mexico had already taken significant steps towards liberalizing its protectionist trade regime.

The U.S.-Canada Free Trade Agreement of 1989

The United States and Canada recently marked the 25th anniversary of the October 3, 1987 signing of the U.S.-Canada Free Trade Agreement (FTA). The FTA was the first economically significant bilateral FTA signed by the United States.[6] Implementing legislation[7] was approved by both Houses of Congress under "fast-track authority"—now known as trade promotion authority (TPA)—and signed by President Ronald Reagan on September 28, 1988. While the FTA generated significant policy debate in the United States, it was a watershed moment for Canada. Controversy surrounding the proposed FTA led to the so-called "free trade election" in 1988, in which sitting Progressive Conservative Prime Minister Brian Mulroney, who negotiated the agreement, defeated Liberal party leader John Turner, who vowed to reject it if elected. After the election, the FTA was passed by Parliament in December 1988, and it came into effect between the two nations on January 1, 1989. At the time, it probably was the most comprehensive bilateral FTA negotiated worldwide and contained several groundbreaking provisions. It:

- Eliminated all tariffs by 1998. Many were eliminated immediately, and the remaining tariffs were phased-out in 5-10 years.

- Continued the 1965 U.S.-Canada Auto Pact, but tightened its rules of origin. Some Canadian auto sector practices not covered by the Auto Pact were ended by 1998.
- Provided national treatment for covered services providers and liberalized financial services trade. Facilitated cross-border travel for business professionals.
- Committed to provide prospective national treatment for investments originating in the other, although established derogations from national treatment such as for national security or prudential reasons were allowed to continue. Banned imposition of performance requirements, such as local content, import substitution, or local sourcing requirements.
- Expanded the size of federal government procurement markets available for competitive bidding from suppliers of the other country. It did not include sub-federal government procurement.
- Provided for a binding binational panel to resolve disputes arising from the agreement (a Canadian insistence).
- Prohibited most import and export restrictions on energy products, including minimum export prices. This was carried forth in NAFTA only with regard to Canada-U.S. energy trade.

Many of these provisions were incorporated into, or expanded in, NAFTA. However, the FTA did not include, or specifically exempted, some issues that would appear in NAFTA for the first time. These include

- *Intellectual property rights (IPR).* The FTA did not contain language on intellectual property rights. NAFTA was the first FTA to include meaningful disciplines on IPR.
- *Cultural exemption.* It exempted the broadcasting, film, and publishing sectors. This exemption continues in NAFTA.
- *Transportation services and investment* in the Canadian energy sector were excluded from the FTA. These exclusions were limited in NAFTA.
- *Trade remedies.* Neither the FTA nor NAFTA ended the use of trade remedy actions (anti-dumping, countervailing duty, or safeguards) against the other. This was a key Canadian goal of the FTA. NAFTA did create a separate dispute settlement mechanism to adjudicate trade

remedy disputes, but this mechanism has not been replicated in other FTAs.

- *Softwood lumber.* The FTA grandfathered in the then-present 1986 Memorandum of Understanding (MOU) governing softwood lumber trade. Over time, the MOU has been replaced by other agreements—such as the current Softwood Lumber Agreement (SLA)—and, at times, by resort to trade remedy actions.
- *Agricultural supply management.* Canada was able to exempt its agriculture supply management system, although it committed to allow a small increase in imports of dairy, poultry, and eggs, which carried over into the NAFTA. The United States was also able to exclude certain products from liberalization commitments under the FTA and the NAFTA.

Mexico's Pre-NAFTA Trade Liberalization Efforts

Well before NAFTA negotiations began, Mexico was already liberalizing its protectionist trade and investment policies that had been in place for decades (see Appendix B for more information on Mexico's pre-NAFTA protectionist policies). The restrictive trade regime began after Mexico's revolutionary period and remained until the early- to mid-1980's when the country was facing a debt crisis. It was at this time that the government took unilateral steps to open and modernize its economy by relaxing investment policies and liberalizing trade barriers. The trade liberalization measures that began in the mid-1980s shifted Mexico from one of the world's most protected economies into one of the most open. Mexico now has 12 FTAs involving 44 countries.[8]

Mexico's first steps in opening its closed economy focused on reforming its import substitution policies in the mid-1980s. Further reforms were made in 1986 when Mexico became a member of the General Agreement on Tariffs and Trade (GATT). As a condition of becoming a GATT member, for example, Mexico agreed to lower its maximum tariff rates to 50%. Mexico went further by reducing its highest tariff rate from 100% to 20%. Mexico's trade-weighted average tariff fell from 25% in 1985 to about 19% in 1989.[9]

Although Mexico had been lowering trade and investment restrictions since 1986, the number of remaining barriers for U.S. exports remained high at the time of the NAFTA negotiations. Mexico required import licenses on 230 products from the United States, affecting about 7% of the value of U.S.

exports to Mexico. Prior to its entry into GATT, Mexico required import licenses on all imports. At the time of the NAFTA negotiations, about 60% of U.S. agricultural exports to Mexico required import licenses. Mexico also had numerous other nontariff barriers, such as "official import prices," an arbitrary customs valuation system that raised duty assessments.[10]

For Mexico, an FTA with the United States represented a way to lock in the reforms of its market opening measures from the mid-1980s to transform Mexico's formerly statist economy after the devastating debt crisis of the 1980s.[11] The combination of the severe economic impact of the debt crisis, low domestic savings, and an increasingly overvalued peso, put pressure on the Mexican government to adopt market-opening economic reforms and boost imports of goods and capital to encourage more competition in the Mexican market. An FTA with the United States was a way of blocking domestic efforts to roll back Mexican reforms, especially in the politically sensitive agriculture sector. NAFTA helped deflect protectionist demands of industrial groups and special interest groups in Mexico.[12] One of the main goals of the Mexican government was to increase investment confidence in order to attract greater flows of foreign investment and spur economic growth. Since the entry into force of NAFTA, Mexico has used the agreement as a basic model for other FTAs Mexico has signed with other countries.[13]

For the United States, NAFTA represented an opportunity to expand the growing export market to the south, but it also represented a political opportunity for the United States and Mexico to work together in resolving some of the tensions in the bilateral relationship.[14] An FTA with Mexico would help U.S. businesses expand exports to a growing market of almost 100 million people. U.S. officials also recognized that imports from Mexico would likely include higher U.S. content than imports from Asian countries. In addition to the trade and investment opportunities that NAFTA represented, an agreement with Mexico would be a way to support the growth of political pluralism and a deepening of democratic processes in Mexico. NAFTA also presented an opportunity for the United States to spur the slow progress on the Uruguay Round of multilateral trade negotiations.[15]

Overview of NAFTA Provisions

At the time that NAFTA was implemented, the U.S.-Canada FTA was already in effect and U.S. tariffs on most Mexican goods were low. NAFTA opened up the U.S. market to increased Mexican imports and the Mexican market to the United States and Canada, creating a single market with 400 million people and accounting for one-third of the world's output of approximately $1 trillion per year.[16] Some of the key NAFTA provisions included tariff and non-tariff trade liberalization, rules of origin, services trade, foreign investment, intellectual property rights protection, government procurement, and dispute resolution. Labor and environmental provisions were included in separate NAFTA side agreements.

Removal of Trade Barriers

The market opening provisions of the agreement gradually eliminated all tariffs and most non-tariff barriers on goods produced and traded within North America over a period of fifteen years after it entered into force. Some tariffs were eliminated immediately, while others were phased out in various schedules of five to fifteen years. U.S. import-sensitive sectors, such as glassware, footwear, and ceramic tile, received longer phase-out schedules.[17] NAFTA provided the option of accelerating tariff reductions if the countries involved agreed.[18] The agreement included safeguard provisions in which the importing country could increase tariffs, or impose quotas in some cases, on imports during a transition period if domestic producers faced serious injury as a result of increased imports from another NAFTA country. It terminated all existing drawback programs by January 1, 2001.[19]

Given that the U.S.-Canada FTA was already in place, most of the market opening measures resulted in the removal of U.S. tariffs and quotas applied to imports from Mexico, and Mexican trade barriers applied to imports from the United States and Canada. At the time that NAFTA went into effect, about 40% of U.S. imports from Mexico entered duty-free and the remainder faced duties of up to 35%, with a trade-weighted average rate of about 7%. Mexico's trade-weighted tariff on U.S. agricultural products averaged about 11%. Also affecting U.S.-Mexico trade were both countries' phytosanitary rules, Mexican import licensing requirements, and U.S. marketing orders.[20]

Some of the more significant changes took place in the textiles, apparel, automotive, and agricultural industries. Elimination of trade barriers in these key industries are summarized below.

- *Textiles and Apparel Industries.* NAFTA phased out all duties on textile and apparel goods within North America meeting specific NAFTA rules of origin[21] over a 10-year period. Prior to NAFTA, 65%

of U.S. apparel imports from Mexico entered duty-free and quota-free, and the remaining 35% faced an average tariff rate of 17.9%. Mexico's average tariff on U.S. textile and apparel products was 16%, with duties as high as 20% on some products.[22]

- *Automotive Industry.* NAFTA phased out Mexico's restrictive auto decree. It phased out all U.S. tariffs imports from Mexico and Mexican tariffs on U.S. and Canadian products as long as they met the rules of origin requirements of 62.5% North American content for autos, light trucks, engines and transmissions; and 60% for other vehicles and automotive parts. Some tariffs were eliminated immediately, while others were phased out in periods of 5 to 10 years. Prior to NAFTA, the United States assessed the following tariffs on imports from Mexico: 2.5% on automobiles, 25% on light-duty trucks, and a trade-weighted average of 3.1% for automotive parts. Mexican tariffs on U.S. and Canadian automotive products were as follows: 20% on automobiles and light trucks, and 10-20% on auto parts.[23]
- *Agriculture.* NAFTA set out separate bilateral undertakings on cross-border trade in agriculture, one between Canada and Mexico, and the other between Mexico and the United States. As a general matter, U.S.-Canada FTA provisions continued to apply on trade with Canada.[24] Regarding U.S.-Mexico agriculture trade, NAFTA eliminated most non-tariff barriers in agricultural trade, either through their conversion to tariff-rate quotas (TRQ's)[25] or ordinary tariffs. Tariffs were phased out over a period of 15 years with sensitive products such as sugar and corn receiving the longest phase-out periods. Approximately one-half of U.S.-Mexico agricultural trade became duty-free when the agreement went into effect. Prior to NAFTA, most tariffs, on average, in agricultural trade between the United States and Mexico were fairly low though some U.S. exports to Mexico faced tariffs as high as 12%. However, approximately one-fourth of U.S. agricultural exports to Mexico (by value) were subjected to restrictive import licensing requirements.[26]

Services Trade Liberalization

NAFTA services provisions established a set of basic rules and obligations in services trade among partner countries. The agreement expanded on initiatives in the U.S.-Canada FTA and the Uruguay Round of multilateral trade negotiations to create internationally-agreed disciplines on government regulation of trade in services.[27] The agreement granted services providers certain rights concerning nondiscriminatory treatment, cross-border sales and entry, investment, and access to information. However, there were certain exclusions and reservations by each country. These included maritime shipping (United States), film and publishing (Canada), and oil and gas drilling (Mexico).[28] Although NAFTA liberalized certain service sectors in Mexico, particularly financial services, which profoundly altered its banking sector, other sectors were barely affected.[29] In telecommunications services, NAFTA partners agreed to exclude provision of, but not the use of, basic telecommunications services. NAFTA granted a "bill of rights" for the providers and users of telecommunications services, including access to public telecommunications services; connection to private lines that reflect economic costs and available on a flat-rate pricing basis; and the right to choose, purchase, or lease terminal equipment best suited to their needs.[30] However, NAFTA did not require parties to authorize a person of another NAFTA country to provide or operate telecommunications transport networks or services. NAFTA did not bar a party from maintaining a monopoly provider of public networks or services, such as Telmex, Mexico's dominant telecommunications company.[31]

Other Provisions

In addition to market opening measures through the elimination of tariff and non-tariff barriers, NAFTA incorporated numerous other provisions, including foreign investment, intellectual property rights (IPR), dispute resolution, and government procurement.

- *Foreign Investment.* NAFTA removed significant investment barriers, ensured basic protections for NAFTA investors, and provided a mechanism for the settlement of disputes between investors and a NAFTA country. NAFTA provided for "non-discriminatory treatment" for foreign investment by NAFTA parties in certain sectors of other NAFTA countries.[32] The agreement included explicit country-specific liberalization commitments and exceptions to national treatment. Exemptions from NAFTA investment provisions include the energy sector in Mexico in which the Mexican government reserved the right to prohibit foreign investment. It also included exceptions related to national security and to Canada's cultural industries.[33]

- *IPR.* NAFTA built upon the then-ongoing Uruguay Round negotiations that would create the Trade Related Aspects of Intellectual Property Rights (TRIPS) agreement in the World Trade Organization and on various existing international intellectual property treaties. The agreement set out specific enforceable commitments by NAFTA parties regarding the protection of copyrights, patents, trademarks, and trade secrets, among other provisions. preventing and settling disputes were built upon provisions in the U.S.-Canada FTA. NAFTA created a system of arbitration for resolving disputes that included initial consultations, taking the issue to the NAFTA Trade Commission, or going through arbitral panel proceedings.[34] NAFTA included separate dispute settlement provisions for addressing disputes over antidumping and countervailing duty determinations.
- *Government Procurement.* NAFTA opened up a significant portion of federal government procurement in each country on a nondiscriminatory basis to suppliers from other NAFTA countries for goods and services. It contains some limitations for procurement by state-owned enterprises.[35]

NAFTA Side Agreements on Labor and the Environment

The NAFTA text did not include labor or environmental provisions, which was a major concern to many in Congress at the time of the agreement's consideration. Some policy makers called for additional provisions to address numerous concerns about labor and environmental issues, specifically in Mexico. Other policy makers argued that the economic growth generated by the FTA would increase Mexico's resources available for environmental and worker rights protection. However, congressional concerns from policy makers, as well as concerns from labor and environmental groups, remained strong.

Shortly after he began his presidency, President Clinton addressed labor and environmental concerns by joining his counterparts in Canada and Mexico in negotiating formal side agreements. The NAFTA implementing legislation included provisions related to the side agreements, authorizing U.S. participation in NAFTA labor and environmental commissions and appropriations for these activities. The North American Agreement on Labor Cooperation (NAALC) and the North American Agreement on Environmental Cooperation (NAAEC) entered into force on January 1, 1994, the same day as NAFTA.[36] NAFTA implementing legislation also included two adjustment assistance programs, designed to ease trade-related labor problems: the NAFTA Transitional Adjustment Assistance (NAFTA-TAA) Program and the U.S. Community Adjustment and Investment Program (USCAIP).

The labor and environmental side agreements included language to promote cooperation on labor and environmental matters as well as provisions to address a party's failure to enforce its own labor and environmental laws. Perhaps most notable were the side agreements' dispute settlement processes that, as a last resort, may impose monetary assessments and sanctions to address a party's failure to enforce its laws.[37] NAFTA marked the first time that labor and environmental provisions were associated with an FTA. For many, it represented an opportunity for cooperating on environmental and labor matters across borders and for establishing a new type of relationship among NAFTA partners.[38]

In addition to the two trilateral side agreements, the United States and Mexico entered into a bilateral side agreement to NAFTA on border environmental cooperation.[39] In this agreement, the two governments committed to cooperate on developing environmental infrastructure projects along the U.S.-Mexico border to address concerns about the degradation of the environment along the U.S.-Mexico border due to increased economic activity. The agreement established two organizations to address these concerns: the Border Environment Cooperation Commission (BECC), located in Juárez, Mexico, and the North American Development Bank (NADBank), located in San Antonio, Texas. The sister organizations work closely together and with other partners at the federal, state and local level in the United States and Mexico to develop, certify, and facilitate financing for water and wastewater treatment, municipal solid waste disposal, and related projects on both sides of the U.S.-Mexico border region. Both organizations also have ongoing efforts to measure the results of the projects on the border region. From 1995 to 2011, BECC certified 189 projects (86 in the United States and 103 in Mexico), representing nearly $4.3 billion in environmental infrastructure investment, directly benefiting 14 million border residents. NADBank has financed 152 of these projects with approximately $1.33 billion in loans and grants.[40] These projects have provided border residents with more access to drinking water, sewer and wastewater treatment. They also include water conservation, air quality, and renewable energy projects.[41]

TRADE TRENDS AND ECONOMIC EFFECTS

Many economists contend that trade liberalization promotes overall economic growth and efficiency among trading partners, although there are short-term adjustment costs. NAFTA was unusual in global terms because it was the first time that an FTA linked two wealthy, developed countries with a low-income developing country. For this reason, the agreement received considerable attention by U.S. policy makers, manufacturers, service providers, agriculture producers, labor unions, non-government organizations, and academics. Proponents argued that the agreement would help generate thousands of jobs and reduce income disparity between Mexico and its northern neighbors. Opponents warned that the agreement would create huge job losses in the United States as companies moved production to Mexico to lower costs.[42]

Estimating the economic impact of trade agreements is a daunting task due to a lack of data and important theoretical and practical matters associated with generating results from economic models. In addition, such estimates provide an incomplete accounting of the total economic effects of trade agreements.[43] Numerous studies suggest that NAFTA achieved many of the intended trade and economic benefits.[44] Other studies suggest that NAFTA has come at a cost to U.S. workers.[45] This has been in keeping with what most economists maintain, that trade liberalization promotes overall economic growth among trading partners, but that there are both winners and losers from adjustments.

Not all changes in trade and investment patterns within North America since 1994 can be attributed to NAFTA because trade has also been affected by a number of factors. The sharp devaluation of the peso at the end of the 1990s and the associated recession in Mexico had considerable effects on trade, as did the rapid growth of the U.S. economy during most of the 1990s and, more recently, the economic slowdown caused by the 2008 financial crisis. Trade-related job gains and losses since NAFTA may have accelerated trends that were ongoing prior to NAFTA and may not be totally attributable to the trade agreement.

U.S. Trade Trends with NAFTA Partners

Overall Trade

U.S. trade with its NAFTA partners has more than tripled since the agreement took effect. It has increased more rapidly than trade with the rest of the world. In 2011, trilateral trade among NAFTA partners reached the $1 trillion threshold. Trade between the United States and Mexico contributed considerably to growth in North American trade, accounting for approximately half of the increase in regional trade since 1994. Between 1993 and 2013, total U.S. trade with Mexico increased by 522%. In comparison, U.S. trade with Canada increased by 200%, while trade with non-NAFTA countries increased by 279%. In 2013, Canada was the leading market for U.S. exports, while Mexico ranked second. The two countries accounted for 33% of total U.S. exports in 2013. In imports, Canada and Mexico ranked second and third, respectively, as suppliers of U.S. imports in 2013. The two countries accounted for 27% of U.S. imports.[46]

Most of the trade-related effects of NAFTA may be attributed to changes in trade and investment patterns with Mexico because economic integration between Canada and the United States had already been taking place. As mentioned previously, while NAFTA may have accelerated U.S.- Mexico trade since 1993, other factors, such as economic growth patterns, also affected trade. As trade tends to increase during cycles of economic growth, it tends to decrease as growth declines.

The economic downturns in 2001 and 2009, for example, likely played a role in the decline in both U.S. exports to and imports from Canada and Mexico, as shown in *Figure 1*.

Energy Trade Implications

Trade in petroleum products is a central component of U.S. trade with both Canada and Mexico. Approximately 16% of total trade with NAFTA partners is in petroleum products. Canada and Mexico accounted for 40% ($108.2 billion) of total U.S. crude oil imports ($273.5 billion) in 2013. Canada is the leading supplier of crude petroleum oil to the United States, followed by Saudi Arabia and Mexico. If petroleum products are excluded from trade statistics, the United States has had a trade surplus with NAFTA partners in merchandise trade since 2011, as shown in *Figure 2*. In 2013, the trade surplus in non-petroleum products was an estimated $9.2 billion.

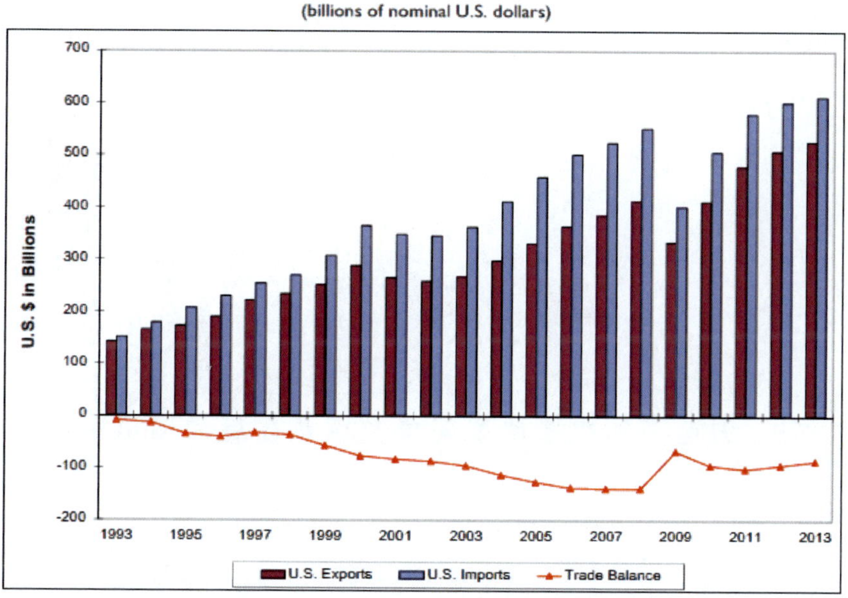

Source: Compiled by CRS using trade data from the U.S. International Trade Commission's Interactive Tariff and Trade Data Web, at http://dataweb.usitc.gov.

Figure 1. U.S. Merchandise Trade with NAFTA Partners: 1993-2013.

Imports in crude petroleum oil rank first among the five leading import items from NAFTA partners, as shown in *Figure 3*.[47] The value of crude oil imports from both Canada and Mexico in 2013 totaled $108.3 billion. Since 2007, crude petroleum imports have ranked first among leading imports from both countries, reaching a high of $109.8 billion in 2012. In 2009, the value of crude oil imports dropped considerably, from $100.1 billion in 2008 to $59.1 billion in 2009, reflecting a drop in oil prices that year.

Trade with Canada

U.S. trade with Canada more than doubled in the first decade of the FTA/NAFTA (1989-1999) from $166.5 billion to $362.2 billion. U.S. exports to Canada increased from $100.2 billion in 1993 to $300.2 billion in 2013, an increase of 200%. U.S. imports from Canada increased from $110.9 billion in 1993 to $332.1 billion in 2013, also a 200% increase (see *Table A-1*).

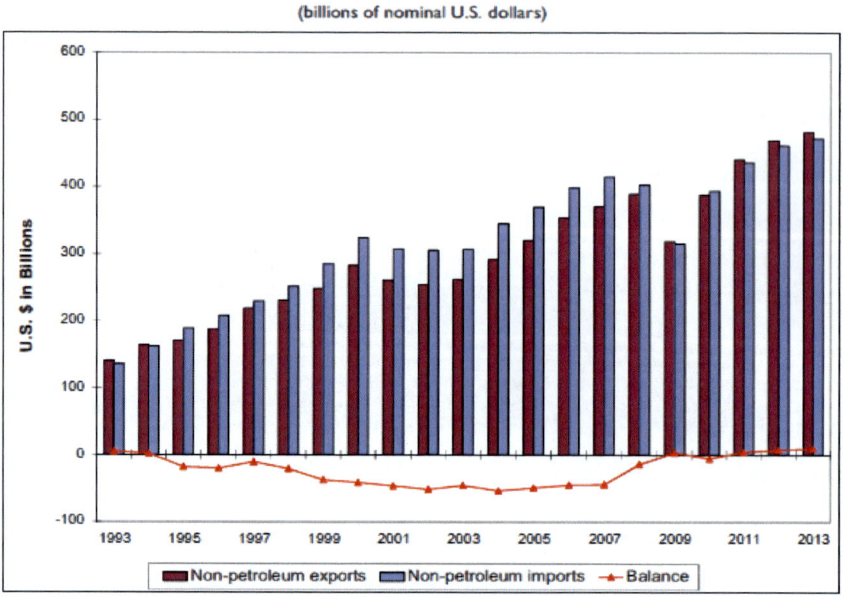

Source: Compiled by CRS using trade data from the U.S. International Trade Commission's (USITC's) Interactive Tariff and Trade Data Web, at http://dataweb.usitc.gov.

Notes: The United States uses different classifications of trade for trade statistics. Trade data in this chart excludes trade in three categories, which include Harmonized Tariff Schedule (HTS) code 2709, petroleum oils and oils from bituminous minerals, crude; HTS code 2710, petroleum oils and oils from bituminous minerals (other than crude) and products therefrom, NESOI, containing 70% (by weight) or more of these oils; and HTS code 2711, petroleum gases and other gaseous hydrocarbons. See http://dataweb.usitc.gov.

Figure 2. Non-Petroleum Trade with NAFTA Partners: 1993-2013.

After falling off during the recession of 2001, total trade with Canada reached a new high of $596.5 billion in 2008, only to fall victim to the financial crisis in 2009 when it fell to $429.6 billion. In 2011, total trade had returned to 2008 levels at $597.3 billion. The United States has run a trade deficit with Canada since the FTA/NAFTA era, increasing from $9.9 billion in 1989 to $74.6 billion in 2008, before falling back during the 2009 recession. In 2013, the trade deficit with Canada was $31.9 billion. While the increase in the trade deficit with Canada has been attributed to the FTA/NAFTA, the increase has been uneven and may also be attributed to other economic factors, such as energy prices.[48]

(HTS 4-digit level)

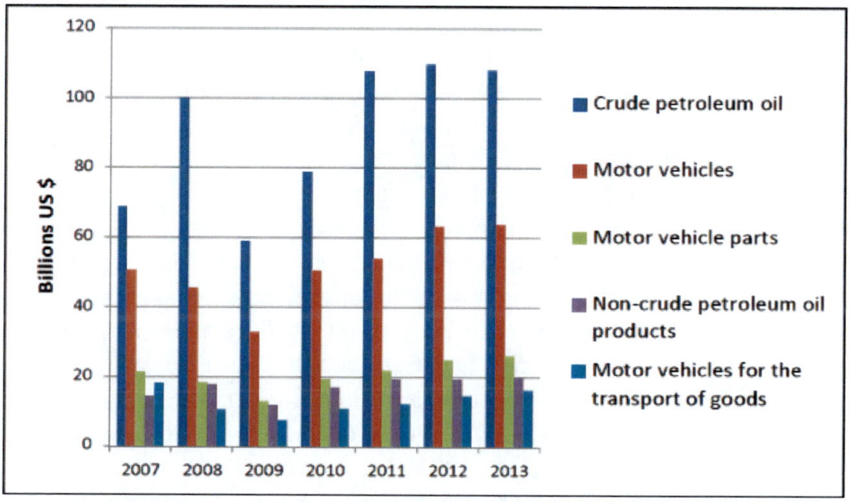

Source: Compiled by CRS using trade data from the USITC at http://dataweb.usitc.gov.

Notes: Statistics in this figure are derived from the Harmonized Tariff Schedule (HTS) of the United States at the 4-digit level. The HTS comprises a hierarchical structure for describing all goods in trade for duty, quota, and statistical purposes. This structure is based upon the international Harmonized Commodity Description and Coding System (HS), administered by the World Customs Organization in Brussels. See http://dataweb.usitc.gov.

Figure 3. Top Five Import Items from NAFTA Partners.

Trade with Mexico

The United States is, by far, Mexico's leading partner in merchandise trade. U.S. exports to Mexico increased rapidly since NAFTA, increasing from $41.6 billion in 1993 to $226.2 billion in 2013, an increase of 444% (see *Table A-1 in Appendix A*). U.S. imports from Mexico increased from $39.9 billion in 1993 to $280.5 billion in 2013, an increase of 603%. The trade balance with Mexico went from a surplus of $1.7 billion in 1993 to a deficit of $61.4 billion in 2012. In 2013, the trade deficit with Mexico decreased to $54.3 billion. Fourteen percent of total U.S. merchandise exports were destined for Mexico and 12% of U.S. merchandise imports came from Mexico.[49] In services, the United States had a surplus of $12.3 billion in 2012 in trade with Mexico. U.S. private services exports to Mexico increased from $10.4 billion in 1993 to $27.4 billion in 2012. U.S. private services imports from Mexico increased from $7.4 billion in 1993 to $15.1 billion in 2012, as shown in *Table A-2*.[50]

NAFTA's Effect on the U.S. Economy

The overall net effect of NAFTA on the U.S. economy has been relatively small, primarily because total trade with both Mexico and Canada was equal to less than 5% of U.S. GDP at the time NAFTA went into effect. Because many, if not most, of the economic effects came as a result of U.S.-Mexico trade liberalization, it is also important to take into account that two-way trade with Mexico was equal to an even smaller percentage of GDP (1.4%) in 1994. Thus, any changes in trade patterns would not be expected to be significant in relation to the overall U.S. economy. A major challenge in assessing NAFTA is separating the effects that came as a result of the agreement from other factors. U.S. trade with Mexico and Canada was already growing prior to NAFTA and it likely would have continued to do so without an agreement. A 2003 report by the Congressional Budget Office observed that it was difficult to precisely measure the effects of NAFTA. It estimated that NAFTA likely increased annual U.S. GDP, but by a very small amount – "probably no more than a few billion dollars, or a few hundredths of a percent."[51] In some sectors, trade-related effects could have been more significant, especially in those industries that were more exposed to the removal of tariff and non-tariff trade barriers, such as the textile, apparel, automotive, and agriculture industries.

Studies by the U.S. International Trade Commission (USITC) on the effects of NAFTA pointed out the difficulty in isolating the agreement's effects from other factors. Although the effects of NAFTA are not easily measured, the USITC provided some estimates over the years. A 2003 study estimated that U.S. GDP could experience an increase between 0.1% and 0.5% upon full implementation of the agreement.[52] Another USITC study that was congressionally mandated in 1997 offered a comprehensive assessment of the operation and effects of NAFTA after three years.[53] The report estimated that NAFTA had a small, but positive, effect on the overall U.S. economy. Some of the findings include the following: data inadequacies at the industry level made it difficult to isolate the effects of NAFTA on absolute trade flows; U.S. trade with NAFTA partners increased more rapidly than U.S. trade with the rest of the world; the share of U.S. exports in the Mexican market increased by a higher percentage than the share of total imports from other countries; industries such as autos, chemicals, textiles, and electronics benefitted by achieving synergies across the North American market.[54]

U.S. Industries and Supply Chains

Many economists and other observers have credited NAFTA with helping U.S. manufacturing industries, especially the U.S. auto industry, become more globally competitive through the development of supply chains.[55] Much of the increase in U.S.-Mexico trade, for example, can be attributed to specialization as manufacturing and assembly plants have reoriented to take advantage of economies of scale. As a result, supply chains have been increasingly crossing national boundaries as manufacturing work is performed wherever it is most efficient.[56] A reduction in tariffs in a given sector not only affects prices in that sector but also in industries that purchase intermediate inputs from that sector. The importance of these direct and indirect effects is often overlooked, according to one study. The study suggests that these linkages offer important trade and welfare gains from free trade agreements and that ignoring these input-output linkages could underestimate potential trade gains.[57]

Much of the trade between the United States and its NAFTA partners occurs in the context of production sharing as manufacturers in each country work together to create goods. The expansion of trade has resulted in the creation of vertical supply relationships, especially along the U.S.-Mexico border. The flow of intermediate inputs produced in the United States and exported to Mexico and the return flow of finished products greatly increased the importance of the U.S.-Mexico border region as a production site.[58] U.S. manufacturing industries, including automotive, electronics, appliances, and machinery, all rely on the assistance of Mexican manufacturers. One report estimates that 40% of the content of U.S. imports from Mexico and 25% of the content of U.S. imports from Canada are of U.S. origin. In comparison, U.S. imports from China are said to have only 4% U.S. content. Taken together, goods from Mexico and Canada represent about 75% of all the U.S. domestic content that returns to the United States as imports.[59]

NAFTA was instrumental in the integration of the North American auto industry, which experienced some of the most significant changes in trade following the agreement. U.S. auto parts producers may use inputs and components produced by another NAFTA partner to assemble parts, which are then shipped to another NAFTA country where they are assembled into a vehicle that is sold in any of the three NAFTA countries.[60] NAFTA provisions consisted of a phased elimination of tariffs and the gradual removal of many non-tariff barriers to trade. It provided for uniform country of origin provisions, enhanced protection of intellectual property rights, adopted less restrictive government procurement practices, and eliminated performance requirements on investors from other NAFTA countries. NAFTA established the removal of Mexico's restrictive trade and investment policies and the elimination of U.S. tariffs on autos and auto parts.

After NAFTA's entry into force, U.S. trade in vehicles and auto parts increased rapidly. Mexico became a more significant trading partner in the U.S. motor vehicle market as U.S. auto exports to Mexico increased 245% while imports increased 587% (see *Table 1*). Mexico's share in U.S. total trade in motor vehicles increased from 5% to 18% between 1993 and 2013, while the share from Canada and other countries decreased. In auto parts, Mexico's share increased from 21% to 36% over the same period. In 2013, Mexico was the leading supplier of automotive goods for the United States, accounting for 28% ($76.3 billion) of total U.S. motor vehicle and auto parts imports. Canada ranked second with 21% ($58.0 billion) of the U.S. market share in 2013.[61]

Table 1. U.S. Trade in Vehicles and Auto Parts: 1993 and 2013 (billions of U.S. dollars)

		1993			*2013*		*% Change 1993-2011*	
	Exports	*Imports*	*Total*	*Exports*	*Imports*	*Total*	*Exports*	*Imports*
Mexico								
Vehicles	0.2	3.7	3.9	4.8	40.1	44.9	2300%	984%
Parts	7.3	7.4	14.7	21.1	36.2	57.3	189%	389%
Total	7.5	11.1	18.6	25.9	76.3	102.2	245%	587%
Canada								
Vehicles	8.2	26.7	34.9	26.2	44.5	70.7	220%	67%
Parts	18.2	10.3	28.5	26.5	13.5	40.0	46%	31%
Total	26.4	37.0	63.4	52.7	58.0	110.7	100%	57%
World								
Vehicles	18.9	63.0	81.9	73.1	175.7	248.8	287%	179%
Parts	33.4	38.3	71.7	60.6	100.4	161.0	81%	162%
Total	52.3	101.3	153.6	133.7	276.1	409.8	156%	173%

Source: Compiled by CRS using trade data from the USITC at http://dataweb.usitc.gov. For 2013, "vehicles" consists of items under the North American Industrial Classification System (NAICS) number 3361 and "parts" consists of items under NAIC number 3363.

Note: The NAICS is the standard used by Federal statistical agencies in classifying business establishments for the purpose of collecting, analyzing, and publishing statistical data related to the U.S. business economy.

A number of studies have found that NAFTA has brought economic and social benefits to the Mexican economy as a whole, but that the benefits have not been evenly distributed throughout the country.[62] The agreement also had a positive impact on Mexican productivity. A 2011 World Bank study found that the increase in trade integration after NAFTA had a positive effect on stimulating the productivity of Mexican plants.[63] Most post-NAFTA studies on economic effects have found that the net overall effects on the Mexican economy tended to be positive but modest. While there have been periods of positive and negative economic growth in Mexico after the agreement was implemented, it is difficult to measure precisely how much of these economic changes were attributed to NAFTA. A World Bank study assessing some of the economic impacts from NAFTA on Mexico concluded that NAFTA helped Mexico get closer to the levels of development in the United States and Canada. The study states that NAFTA helped Mexican manufacturers adapt to U.S. technological innovations more quickly; likely had positive impacts on the number and quality of jobs; reduced macroeconomic volatility, or wide variations in the GDP growth rate, in Mexico; increased the levels of synchronicity in business cycles in Mexico, the United States, and Canada; and reinforced the high sensitivity of Mexican economic sectors to economic developments in the United States.[64]

Other studies suggest that NAFTA has been disappointing in that it failed to significantly improve the Mexican economy or lower income disparities between Mexico and its northern neighbors.[65] Some argue that the success of NAFTA in Mexico was probably limited by the fact that NAFTA was not supplemented by complementary policies that could have promoted a deeper regional integration effort. These policies could have included improvements in education, industrial policies, and/or investment in infrastructure.[66]

One of the more controversial aspects of NAFTA is related to the agricultural sector in Mexico and the perception that NAFTA has caused a higher amount of worker displacement in this sector than in other economic sectors. Many critics of NAFTA say that the agreement led to severe job displacement in agriculture, especially in the corn sector. One study estimates these losses to have been over a million lost jobs in corn production between 1991 and 2000.[67] However, while some of the changes in the agricultural sector are a direct result of NAFTA as Mexico began to import more lower-priced products from the United States, many of the changes can be attributed to Mexico's unilateral agricultural reform measures in the 1980s and early 1990s. Most domestic reform measures consisted of privatization efforts and resulted in increased competition. Measures included eliminating state enterprises related to agriculture and removing staple price supports and subsidies.[68] These reforms coincided with NAFTA negotiations and continued beyond the implementation of NAFTA in 1994. The unilateral reforms in the agricultural sector make it difficult to separate those effects from the effects of NAFTA.

U.S.-Mexico Trade Market Shares

Mexico relies heavily on the United States as an export market; this reliance has diminished very slightly over the years. The percentage of Mexico's total exports going to the United States decreased from 83% in 1993 to 78% in 2012 (see *Figure 4*). In addition, its share of the U.S. market has lost ground since 2003 when China surpassed Mexico as the second-leading supplier of U.S. imports. The United States is losing market share of Mexico's import market. Between 1993 and 2012, the U.S. share of Mexico's imports decreased from 78% to 55%. China is Mexico's second-leading source of imports.

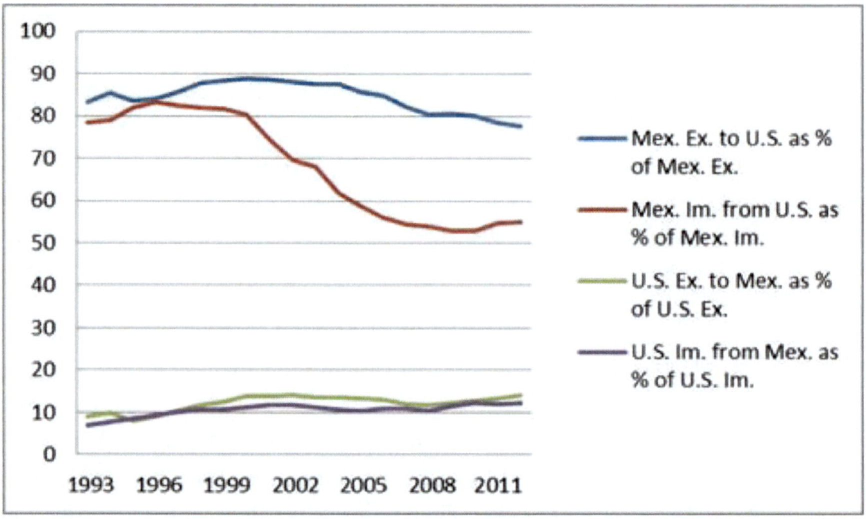

Source: Economist Intelligence Unit, from IMF International Financial Statistics.

Notes: Represents exports to and imports from other country as percentage of country's total trade. Statistics prior to 1993 are not available.

Figure 4. Market Share as Percentage of Total Trade: Mexico and the United States. (1993-2012).

U.S. and Mexican Foreign Direct Investment

Foreign direct investment (FDI) has been an integral part of the economic relationship between the United States and Mexico for many years, especially after NAFTA. Two-way investment increased rapidly after the agreement went into effect. The United States is the largest source of FDI in Mexico. The stock of U.S. FDI in Mexico increased from $15.2 billion in 1993 to $101.0 billion in 2012, a 564% increase (see *Table A-4 in Appendix A*). The flows of FDI have been affected by other factors over the years, with higher growth during the period of economic expansion during the late 1990s, and slower growth in recent years, possibly due to the economic downturn caused by the 2008 global financial crisis and/or the increased violence in Mexico. Mexican FDI in the United States, while substantially lower than U.S. investment in Mexico, has also increased rapidly, from $1.2 billion in 1993 to $14.9 billion in 2012, an increase of over 1000% (See *Table A-4*).[69]

While Mexico's unilateral trade and investment liberalization measures in the 1980s and early 1990s contributed to the increase of U.S. FDI in Mexico, NAFTA provisions on foreign investment may have helped to lock in Mexico's reforms and increase investor confidence. NAFTA helped give U.S. and Canadian investors nondiscriminatory treatment of their investments as well as investor protection in Mexico. Nearly half of total FDI investment in Mexico is in the manufacturing industry.

Income Disparity

One of the main arguments in favor of NAFTA at the time it was being proposed by policy makers was that the agreement would improve economic conditions in Mexico and narrow the income disparity between Mexico and the United States and Canada. Studies that have addressed the issue of economic convergence[70] have noted that economic convergence in North America has failed to materialize. One study states that NAFTA failed to fulfill the promise of closing the Mexico-U.S. development gap and that this was partially due to the lack of deeper forms of regional integration or cooperation between Mexico and the United States.[71] The study contends that domestic policies in both countries, along with underlying geographic and demographic realities, contribute to the continuing disparities in income. The authors argue that neither Mexico nor the United States adopted complementary policies after NAFTA that could have promoted a more successful regional integration effort. These policies could include education, industrial policies, and more investment in border and transportation infrastructure. The authors also note that other developments, such as increased security along the U.S.-Mexico border after the September 11 terrorist attacks, have made it much more difficult for the movement of goods and services across the border and for improving regional integration. They argue that the two countries could cooperate on policies that foster convergence and economic development in Mexico instead of increasing security and "building walls."[72]

A World Bank study states that NAFTA brought economic and social benefits to the Mexican economy, but that it is not enough to help narrow the disparities in economic conditions between Mexico and the United States.[73] It contends that Mexico needs to invest more in education, innovation and infrastructure, and in the quality of national institutions. The study also states that income convergence between a Latin American country and the United States is limited by the wide differences in the quality of domestic institutions, in the innovation dynamics of domestic firms, and in the skills of the labor force. While NAFTA had a positive effect on wages and employment in some Mexican states, the wage differential within the country increased as a result of trade liberalization.[74] Another study also notes that the ability of Mexico to improve economic conditions depends on its capacity to improve its national institutions, adding that Mexican institutions did not improve significantly more than those of other Latin American countries since NAFTA went into effect.[75]

Effect on Canada

As noted earlier, the U.S.-Canada FTA came into effect on January 1, 1989. Thus, trade liberalization between the two countries was well underway—or already completed—by the time of the implementation of NAFTA. This section summarizes the effect of trade liberalization from both agreements on Canada.

From the Canadian perspective, the important consequence of the FTA may have been what did not happen, that is, that many of the fears of opening up trade with the United States did not come to pass. Canada did not become an economic appendage or "51st state" as many had feared. It did not lose control over its water or energy resources; its manufacturing sector was not gutted. Rather, as one Canadian commentator remarked, "free trade helped Canada to grow up, to turn its face out to the world, to embrace its future as a trading nation, [and] to get over its chronic sense of inferiority."[76] However, some hopes for the FTA, for example, that it would be a catalyst for greater productivity in Canadian industry, also have not come to pass.

U.S.-Canada Trade Market Shares

The United States is the number one purchaser of Canadian goods and supplier of imports to Canada. Canada's share of its exports going to the United States steadily increased during the 1980s, from 60.6% in 1980 to 70.7% in 1989, the first year of the FTA. Canada's percentage of total exports to the United States continued to increase, reaching 87.7% in 2002. The relative importance of the value of U.S. and Canadian trade with each other, however, has been falling in recent years. Since 2002, this percentage has steadily fallen back to 74.5% in 2012. The U.S. share of Canada's total imports, which reached a peak of 70.0% in 1983, topped out at 68.7% during the free trade era and has been steadily dropping ever since to a low of 50.6% in 2012 (see *Figure 5*).

Traditionally, Canada was the largest purchaser of U.S. exports and supplier of U.S. imports; however, shares of both peaked before the free trade era. Canada purchased 23.5% of U.S. exports in 1987 and equaled that figure in 2005, but it has since fallen off to 18.9% in 2012. Canada traditionally was the largest supplier of U.S. imports, peaking at 20.6% in 1984, reaching a NAFTA high of 20.1% in 1996, but has declined thereafter to 14.4% in 2012. China displaced Canada as the largest supplier of U.S. imports in 2007.

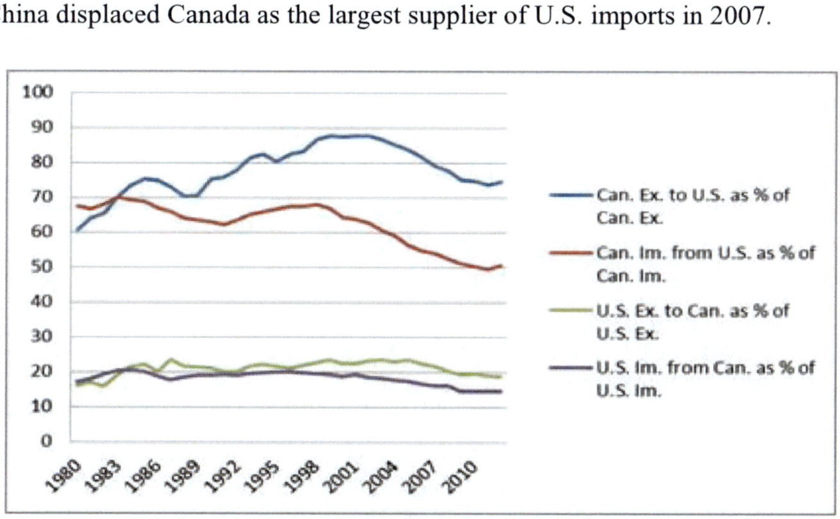

Source: Economic Intelligence Unit, from IMF International Financial Statistics.

Note: Represents exports to and imports from other country as percentage of country's total trade.

Figure 5. Market Share as Percentage of Total Trade: Canada and the United States. (1980-2012).

The composition of trade has also changed. Canada initially entered a manufacturing recession after the conclusion of the FTA as branch plants of U.S. companies set up behind the Canadian tariff wall were abandoned. However, more internationally competitive manufacturing sectors thrived as long as the Canadian dollar (nicknamed the loonie for the soaring loon pictured on its reverse) was relatively cheap. From a low point of a Canadian dollar worth US$0.65 in 2002, the loonie reached parity in 2007, and has hovered around the parity point until 2013 before sliding to a recent US$0.92. The appreciation has been attributed to the boom in Canada's natural resources—oil and gas displaced motor vehicles as Canada's largest export to the United States in 2005. The "great recession" and the woes of the integrated North American auto sector also took a toll on Canadian manufacturing.

For some advocates in Canada, free trade was meant to alleviate the long-term labor productivity gap between the United States and Canada. Open competition was seen as forcing Canadian industry to be more productive. In much of the free trade era, this gap could be accounted for by the low value of the Canadian dollar. As adding capital equipment (often purchased from the United States) was relatively more expensive than hiring extra workers, the latter was often employed. The appreciation of the Canadian dollar has made additional capitalization more attractive, but labor productivity recently remained only at 72% of U.S. levels.[77] The relatively low productivity levels of Canadian industry, as well as its relatively low investments in research and development (R&D), and relatively lower expenditures on information technology, are seen as threatening to Canadian long-term competitiveness, and remain of concern to Canadian policy makers, despite leading the organization of Economic Cooperation and Development's ranking of the population with post-secondary education.[78]

U.S. and Canadian Foreign Direct Investment

Two-way investment has also increased markedly during the free trade era, both in terms of stock and flow of investment. The United States is the largest single investor in Canada with a stock of FDI into Canada reaching $351.5 billion in 2012, up from a stock of $69.9 billion in 1993 (see *Table A-4*). U.S. investment represents nearly 51.5% of the total stock of FDI in Canada from global investors. U.S. FDI flows into Canada averaged $3.28 billion in the five years prior to the FTA, and actually fell to an average of $1.7 billion in the first six years of the FTA, mainly attributed to divestments of U.S.-owned branch plants in Canada. However, U.S. flows into Canada increased markedly to an average of $14.9 billion during the years 1995 to

2012.[79] The stock of U.S. FDI is now equivalent to 18% of the value of Canadian GDP, in contrast to 1% at the beginning of the FTA.

While Canada is not the largest investor in the United States, the United States was the largest destination for Canadian FDI in 2012 with a stock of $225.3 billion, an increase from $26.6 billion in 1988.[80] Approximately 40.7% of Canadian FDI was invested in the United States in 2012. Canadian FDI flows into the United States annually averaged $2.3 billion in five years prior to the FTA, and an annual average of $1.8 billion during the FTA years, but increased to an annual average of $9.9 billion from 1995 to 2012.[81] These trends highlight the changing view of FDI among Canadians, from one that could be considered fearful or hostile to FDI as vehicles of foreign control over the Canadian economy, to one that is more welcoming of new jobs and techniques that result from FDI.

ISSUES FOR CONGRESS

Many economists and business representatives generally look at NAFTA as a success and credit it for fueling unprecedented North American trade and creating job growth in the United States. They look to build on NAFTA's momentum to improve trade relations and economic integration within the region. However, labor groups and some consumer-advocacy groups argue that the agreement has had negative effects. They maintain that the agreement resulted in outsourcing and lower wages that have had a negative effect on the U.S. economy and that it has caused job dislocations in Mexico, especially in agriculture.[82]

Given the increasing number of regional trade agreements throughout the world and the ongoing Trans-Pacific Partnership (TPP) free trade negotiations, one general question that policy makers may consider in forming future trade policy is whether or not NAFTA has lost its relevance. The numerous FTAs that the United States, Mexico, and Canada have put into effect have given other countries the same preferences to the U.S. market that Canada and Mexico benefit from under NAFTA. Similarly, these FTAs have lessened the preferences the United States has in other markets.

Both proponents and critics of NAFTA agree that the three countries should look at what the agreement has failed to do as they look to the future of North American trade and economic relations. Policies could include strengthening institutions to protect the environment and worker rights; considering the establishment of a border infrastructure plan; increasing regulatory cooperation; promoting research and development to enhance the global competiveness of North American industries; investing in more border infrastructure to make border crossings more efficient; and/or creating more efforts to lessen income differentials within the region.

Trans-Pacific Partnership (TPP)

In December 2012, Canada and Mexico began participating in the ongoing negotiations for a proposed TPP free trade agreement (FTA) among 12 countries in the Asia-Pacific region.[83] The United States is an active participant in the negotiations and was among the first tranche of countries to join the original four members of the Trans-Pacific Strategic Economic Partnership (Brunei, Chile, New Zealand, and Singapore) to launch the TPP negotiations in the fall of 2008. With 26 negotiating groups and 29 chapters under discussion, the TPP partners envision the agreement to be "comprehensive and high-standard," in that they seek to eliminate tariffs and non-tariff barriers to trade in goods, services, and agriculture, and to establish rules on a wide range of issues, including intellectual property rights, foreign direct investment and other economic activities. They also strive to create a "21st century agreement" that addresses new and cross-cutting issues presented by an increasingly globalized economy.

The United States has indicated that it is only negotiating bilateral market access in the TPP talks with countries with which it does not have FTAs—Brunei, Japan, Malaysia, New Zealand, and Vietnam. The addition of Japan to the negotiations in the summer of 2013 may afford all three NAFTA countries with the possibility of additional market opening opportunities. However, the United States has sought to go beyond current U.S. FTAs in its proposed rules chapters. This has become a point of contention in the talks and may become an issue for Canada and Mexico as well. The TPP may have implications for NAFTA in several areas, including intellectual property rights (IPR), investment, services, government procurement, as well as labor and environmental provisions. The related provisions in more recent free trade agreements that the United States has negotiated, such as those with Colombia, Panama, Peru, and South Korea, include commitments that go beyond NAFTA. If agreement is reached on a TPP, Canada and Mexico may have to adhere to stronger and more enforceable labor and environmental provisions, stronger IPR provisions, as well as some issues that were not addressed in detail in the NAFTA, such as disciplines on state-owned enterprises.

Regulatory Cooperation

Policy makers may consider issues on how the United States can improve cooperation with its North American neighbors in the areas of trade, transportation, competitiveness, economic growth, and security enhancement. The United States, Canada, and Mexico have made efforts since 2005 to increase cooperation on these issues through various endeavors, most notably by participating in trilateral summits known as the North American Leaders Summits. The most recent Summit took place on February 19, 2014, in Toluca, Mexico. President Barack Obama met with Mexican President Enrique Peña Nieto and Canadian Prime Minister Stephen Harper to discuss the economic well-being of the region; education initiatives; energy and climate change; citizen security; and regional, global, and stakeholder outreach.[84]

After the first North American Leaders' Summit on March 23, 2005 in Waco, TX, the three countries agreed on enhancing regulatory cooperation through the former initiative known as the Security and Prosperity Partnership of North America (SPP). The main goal was to increase and enhance prosperity in the United States, Canada, and Mexico through regulatory cooperation.[85] The Obama Administration has affirmed its commitment to continue past efforts on North American cooperation but under a different approach from the SPP initiative. While these efforts have served as mechanisms to increase communications on issues of mutual interest, their role has been limited because there are no binding agreements.

The former SPP initiative evolved to other efforts pursued by the Obama Administration for regulatory cooperation, which have included separate bilateral endeavors. For example, in May 2010, the United States and Mexico released the Declaration Concerning Twenty-first Century Border Management and, in December 2011, the United States and Canada announced the Beyond the Border Action Plan: A Shared Vision for Perimeter Security and Economic Competiveness. In February 2012, the United States and Mexico announced the High-Level Regulatory Cooperation Council (HLRCC) to help align regulatory principles, an effort similar to the U.S.-Canada Regulatory Cooperation Council. In March 2012, the Defense Ministers of the three countries met in Ottawa, Canada, for the first ever "Trilateral Meetings of North American Defense Ministers" to increase cooperation on national security issues.

Some critics of North American trilateral cooperation contend that the efforts are an attempt to create a common market or economic union in North

America. Others contend that past efforts under the SPP were contributing to the creation of a so-called "NAFTA Superhighway" that would link the United States, Canada, and Mexico with a "super-corridor."[86] Proponents of North American competitiveness and security cooperation view the initiatives as constructive to addressing issues of mutual interest and benefit for all three countries. Business groups generally support increased North American cooperation and believe that it is necessary to enhance the competitiveness of U.S. businesses in the global market.

Proposals for Deeper Regional Integration

The rising number of regional trade agreements throughout the world, in addition to the rising presence of China in Latin America, could have implications for U.S. trade policy with its NAFTA partners beyond the proposed TPP. Some trade policy experts contend that a deepening of economic relations with Canada and Mexico will help promote a common trade agenda with shared values. In addition to economic effects, forming deeper trade and investment ties would have positive implications for corporate governance, labor rights, environmental protection, and democratic governance.[87]

Some policy experts emphasize the importance of North American trade in intermediate goods and supply chains. They argue that the governments of the three countries should improve cooperation in this area and invest more in improving border infrastructure. The increased security measures that began after September 11, 2001 have resulted in a disruption in production chains due to extended and unpredictable wait times along the border. This has disproportionately hurt small and medium sized businesses.[88] The United States and Mexico have recognized the need to enhance cooperation on prioritizing the economic relationship and security and have developed the Twenty-First Century Border Initiative for this purpose.[89] While the initiative has resulted in improvements along the border, some observers contend that policy makers could devote more energy to improving cooperation and enhancing efficiency in cross-border trade.

Other experts have proposed ideas to address ongoing problems in the region and make North American industries more competitive. Some proposals that have emerged include calls for rethinking the current trade relationship under NAFTA by broadening the scope of North American integration and cooperation. One idea, for example, is to develop a North American Investment

Fund to help close the income gap between Mexico and its northern neighbors. The proposed fund would be administered by the World Bank and used to fund infrastructure projects to connect the south of Mexico to the United States and Canada, and also to improve postsecondary education in Mexico.[90] Other ideas are to set up a Customs Union in North America, such as that of the European Union, with a common external tariff to facilitate trade and deepen North American integration; develop a cooperative approach on immigration; and promote regulatory convergence.[91] The proponents of these ideas admit that it would be very difficult for Congress to approve these proposals in the near future, but argue that it is important to think about such options based on the increasing interdependence among NAFTA partners and common interests concerning the future of the region.

APPENDIX A. U.S. MERCHANDISE TRADE WITH NAFTA PARTNERS

Table A-1. U.S. Merchandise Trade with NAFTA Partners (billions of nominal U.S. dollars)

		Canada			Mexico			Total NAFTA	
Year	Exports	Imports	Trade Balance	Exports	Imports	Trade Balance	Exports	Imports	Trade Balance
1993	100.2	110.9	-10.7	41.6	39.9	1.7	141.8	150.8	-9.0
1994	114.3	128.9	-14.6	50.8	49.5	1.3	165.1	178.4	-13.3
1995	126.0	145.1	-19.1	46.3	61.7	-15.4	172.3	206.8	-34.5
1996	132.6	156.5	-23.9	56.8	73.0	-16.2	189.4	229.5	-40.1
1997	150.1	168.1	-18	71.4	85.9	-14.5	221.5	254.0	-32.5
1998	154.2	174.8	-20.6	79.0	94.7	-15.7	233.2	269.5	-36.3
1999	163.9	198.3	-34.4	87.0	109.7	-22.7	250.9	308.0	-57.1
2000	176.4	229.2	-52.8	111.7	135.9	-24.2	288.1	365.1	-77.0
2001	163.7	217.0	-53.3	101.5	131.4	-29.9	265.2	348.4	-83.2
2002	160.8	210.6	-49.8	97.5	134.7	-37.2	258.3	345.3	-87.0
2003	169.5	224.2	-54.7	97.5	138.1	-40.6	267.0	362.3	-95.3
2004	187.7	255.9	-68.2	110.8	155.8	-45	298.5	411.7	-113.2
2005	211.4	287.9	-76.5	120.0	170.2	-50.2	331.4	458.1	-126.7
2006	230.3	303.4	-73.1	134.2	198.3	-64.1	364.5	501.7	-137.2
2007	248.4	313.1	-64.7	136.5	210.8	-74.3	384.9	523.9	-139.0
2008	260.9	335.6	-74.7	151.5	215.9	-64.4	412.4	551.5	-139.1
2009	204.7	224.9	-20.2	129.0	176.5	-47.5	333.7	401.4	-67.7
2010	248.2	276.5	-28.3	164.3	229.7	-65.4	412.5	506.2	-93.7
2011	280.8	316.5	-35.7	197.5	263.1	-65.6	478.3	579.6	-101.3

Table A-1. (Continued)

		Canada			Mexico			Total NAFTA	
Year	Exports	Imports	Trade Balance	Exports	Imports	Trade Balance	Exports	Imports	Trade Balance
2012	291.8	324.2	-32.4	216.3	277.7	-61.4	508.1	601.9	-93.8
2013	300.2	332.1	-31.9	226.2	280.5	-54.3	526.4	612.5	-86.1

Source: Compiled by CRS using trade data from the U.S. International Trade Commission's Interactive Tariff and Trade Data Web, at http://dataweb.usitc.gov.

Table A-2. U.S. Private Services Trade with NAFTA Partners (billions of nominal U.S. dollars)

		Canada			Mexico			Total NAFTA	
Year	Exports	Imports	Services Trade Balance	Exports	Imports	Services Trade Balance	Exports	Imports	Services Trade Balance
1993	17.0	9.1	7.9	10.4	7.4	3.0	27.4	16.5	10.9
1994	17.2	9.9	7.3	11.3	7.9	3.4	28.5	17.8	10.7
1995	17.9	11.0	6.9	8.7	7.9	0.8	26.6	18.9	7.7
1996	19.5	12.4	7.1	9.4	8.9	0.5	28.9	21.3	7.6
1997	20.5	13.7	6.8	10.8	9.9	0.9	31.3	23.6	7.7
1998	19.4	15.0	4.4	11.7	9.8	1.9	31.1	24.8	6.3
1999	22.7	16.2	6.5	14.1	9.4	4.7	36.8	25.6	11.2
2000	24.6	17.9	6.7	15.5	10.8	4.7	40.1	28.7	11.4
2001	24.4	17.4	7.0	16.4	10.4	6.0	40.8	27.8	13.0
2002	25.0	18.0	7.0	17.4	11.6	5.8	42.4	29.6	12.8
2003	27.3	19.6	7.7	18.2	12.1	6.1	45.5	31.7	13.8
2004	29.5	20.7	8.8	19.2	13.6	5.6	48.7	34.3	14.4
2005	32.6	22.0	10.6	22.4	14.2	8.2	55.0	36.2	18.8
2006	37.6	23.2	14.4	23.7	14.6	9.1	61.3	37.8	23.5
2007	42.5	25.0	17.5	24.9	15.2	9.7	67.4	40.2	27.2
2008	44.9	25.1	19.8	25.9	15.5	10.4	70.8	40.6	30.2
2009	43.1	22.9	20.2	22.6	13.6	9.0	65.7	36.5	29.2
2010	52.5	26.5	26.0	24.4	13.6	10.8	76.9	40.1	36.8
2011	58.4	28.4	30.0	25.6	13.9	11.7	84.0	42.3	41.7
2012	61.2	29.8	31.4	27.4	15.1	12.3	88.6	44.9	43.7

Source: Compiled by CRS using data from the Bureau of Economic Analysis online database at http://www.bea.gov.

Table A-3. U.S. Trade with NAFTA Partners by Major Product Category: 2013 (billions of nominal U.S. dollars)

NAFTA Partner	U.S. Exports Leading Items (NAIC 4-digit level)	Value	U.S. Imports Leading Items (NAIC 4-digit level)	Value
Canada	Motor vehicle parts	26.5	Oil and gas	87.6
	Motor vehicles	26.2	Motor vehicles	44.5
	Petroleum and coal products	14.9	Petroleum and coal products	18.7
	Agriculture and construction machinery	11.9	Motor vehicle parts	13.5
	Other general purpose machinery	9.5	Nonferrous metal and processing	10.8
	All Other	211.2	All Other	157.0
	Total exports to Canada	300.2	Total imports from Canada	332.1
Mexico	Motor vehicle parts	21.1	Motor vehicles	40.1
	Petroleum and coal products	19.3	Motor vehicle parts	36.2
	Computer equipment	14.8	Oil and gas	32.0
	Semiconductors and other electronic components	13.0	Computer equipment	14.8
	Basic chemicals	10.1	Audio and video equipment	13.8
	All other	147.9	All other	143.6
	Total Exports to Mexico	226.2	Total Imports from Mexico	280.5

Source: Compiled by CRS using trade data from the U.S. International Trade Commission's Interactive Tariff and Trade Data Web, at http://dataweb.usitc.gov.

Notes: The North American Industrial Classification System (NAICS) is the standard used by federal statistical agencies in classifying business establishments for the purpose of collecting, analyzing, and publishing statistical data related to the U.S. business economy.

Table A-4. U.S. Foreign Direct Investment Positions with Canada and Mexico (1993-2012 historical cost basis [millions of U.S. dollars])

Year	Canadian FDI in the U.S.	U.S. FDI in Canada	Mexican FDI in the U.S.	U.S. FDI in Mexico
1993	40,373	69,922	1,244	15,221
1994	41,219	74,221	2,069	16,968
1995	45,618	83,498	1,850	16,873
1996	54,836	89,592	1,641	19,351
1997	65,175	96,626	3,100	24,050
1998	72,696	98,200	2,055	26,657

Table A-4. (Continued)

Year	Canadian FDI in the U.S.	U.S. FDI in Canada	Mexican FDI in the U.S.	U.S. FDI in Mexico
1999	90,559	119,590	1,999	37,151
2000	114,309	132,472	7,462	39,352
2001	92,420	152,601	6,645	52,544
2002	92,529	166,473	7,829	56,303
2003	95,707	187,953	9,022	56,851
2004	125,276	214,931	7,592	63,384
2005	165,667	231,836	3,595	73,687
2006	165,281	205,134	5,310	82,965
2007	201,924	250,642	8,478	91,046
2008	168,746	246,483	8,420	87,443
2009	188,943	265,326	11,111	82,286
2010	188,943	289,535	11,267	84,288
2011	210,864	318,964	13,763	91,402
2012	225,331	351,460	14,883	101,030

Source: Compiled by CRS using data from the Bureau of Economic Analysis online database at http://www.bea.gov.

APPENDIX B. MEXICO'S PROTECTIONIST TRADE POLICIES PRIOR TO NAFTA

Summary of Mexico's Protectionist Policies Prior to NAFTA

For decades prior to NAFTA Mexico relied on import substitution policies, restrictions on foreign investment, and a controlled exchange rate to help foster domestic growth and to protect itself from a perceived risk of foreign domination.

State-Owned Enterprises (SOEs). Mexico had a strong state presence prior to NAFTA. During the late 1950s and 1960s, the number of state-owned enterprises in Mexico almost doubled from 144 to 272. By 1982, the number of SOES had increased to 1,155. Mexico's economic reforms and divestiture of the state owned sector that occurred during the period of 1983 to 1993 decreased the number of SOEs to 258. By the end of 2003, the number of SOEs dropped to 210.

Import Licenses. Mexico had import license requirements on most, if not all, Mexican imports. The government began to phase these out in the mid-1980s.

By the time NAFTA negotiations started, import licenses were required on only 230 products of the nearly 12,000 items in the Mexican tariff schedule. In agricultural goods, 60% of U.S. exports to Mexico required import licenses or faced other nontariff barriers. There was also a lack of transparency of procedures through which exporters to Mexico could apply for the proper license, certificate, or test.

Foreign Investment Restrictions. Mexico's restrictive Law to Promote Mexican Investment and Regulate Foreign Investment was in effect at the time of NAFTA negotiations, though Mexico had started liberalizing some restrictions in the mid-1980s. In 1991, 37% of Mexican economic activity was not open to 100% foreign investment ownership.

Auto Industry Import Substitution Policy (Auto Decrees). Mexico had a restrictive import substitution policy that began in the 1960s through a series of Mexican Auto Decrees in which the government sought to supply the entire Mexican market through domestically-produced automotive goods. The decrees established import tariffs as high as 25% on automotive goods and had high restrictions on foreign auto production in Mexico. The decrees prohibited imports of finished vehicles; imposed high domestic-content requirements on foreign manufacturers producing cars in Mexico; issued export requirements in which a certain amount of exports was required for every dollar of imports. The government issued the final decree in 1989, after joining the GATT, liberalizing rules on the industry but not entirely eliminating them. Auto manufacturers were still required to have a certain percentage of domestic content in their products and meet export requirements, both of which were considered huge impediments to the industry. Even after joining the GATT, Mexico had tariffs of 20% or more on imports of automobiles and auto parts.

Restrictions in Agriculture. In the period after the 1910 revolution and until the 1980s, Mexico had a land distribution system in which land was redistributed from wealthy land owners and managed by the government. This *ejido* system, formed under Mexico's Agrarian Law, changed in the 1980s when the government began to implement agricultural and trade policy reform measures. Changes included the privatization of the *ejido* system in order to stimulate competition. Mexico's unilateral reform measures included eliminating state enterprises related to agriculture and removing staple price supports and subsidies. Mexico also had a government agency known as CONASUPO which intervened in the agriculture sector. The agency bought staples from farmers at guaranteed prices and processed the products or sold them at low prices to processors and consumers.

Many of Mexico's domestic reforms in agriculture coincided with NAFTA negotiations, beginning in 1991, and continued beyond the implementation of NAFTA in 1994.

The unilateral reforms in the agricultural sector make it difficult to separate those effects from the effects of NAFTA. By 1999, CONASUPO had been abolished.

Sources: United States International Trade Commission (USITC), The Likely Impact on the United States of a Free Trade Agreement with Mexico, Publication 2353, February 1991.Gary Clyde Hufbauer and Jeffrey J. Schott, Institute for International Economics, NAFTA Revisited, October 2005. Alberto Chong and Florencio López-de-Silanes, Privatization in Mexico, Inter-American Development Bank, Working Paper #513, August 2004.

End Notes

[1] See CRS Report R42694, The Trans-Pacific Partnership (TPP) Negotiations and Issues for Congress, coordinated by Ian F. Fergusson.

[2] Trade Promotion Authority, formerly called "fast-track authority" is the authority Congress grants to the President to enter into certain reciprocal trade agreements, and to have their implementing bills considered under expedited legislative procedures, provided the President observes certain statutory obligations. For more information, see CRS Report RL33743, Trade Promotion Authority (TPA) and the Role of Congress in Trade Policy, by William H. Cooper.

[3] Gary Clyde Hufbauer and Jeffrey J. Schott, NAFTA Revisited: Achievements and Challenges, Institute for International Economics, October 2005, Chapter 1.

[4] Pardee Center Task Force Report, The Future of North American Trade Policy: Lessons from NAFTA, Boston University, November 2009.

[5] The Canada-United States Automotive Products Agreement removed tariffs on cars, trucks, buses, tires, and automotive parts between the two countries. NAFTA effectively superseded this agreement.

[6] Prior to the U.S.-Canada FTA, the only bilateral U.S. FTA was with Israel.

[7] United States-Canada Free-Trade Agreement Implementation Act of 1988 (P.L. 100-449)

[8] See CRS Report R40784, Mexico's Free Trade Agreements, by M. Angeles Villarreal.

[9] United States International Trade Commission (USITC), The Likely Impact on the United States of a Free Trade Agreement with Mexico, Publication 2353, February 1991.

[10] Ibid., pp. 1-2.

[11] Gary Clyde Hufbauer and Jeffrey J. Schott, NAFTA Revisited: Achievements and Challenges, Institute for International Economics, October 2005.

[12] Ibid.

[13] Mexico has a total of 12 free trade agreements involving 44 countries. These include agreements with most countries in the Western Hemisphere including the United States, Canada, Chile, Colombia, Costa Rica, Nicaragua, Peru, Guatemala, El Salvador, and Honduras. In addition, Mexico has negotiated FTAs outside of the Western Hemisphere and entered into agreements with Israel, Japan, and the European Union.

[14] Hufbauer and Schott, NAFTA Revisited: Achievements and Challenges, pp. 2-3.

[15] Ibid.

[16] Woodrow Wilson International Center for Scholars, NAFTA at 10: Progress, Potential, and Precedents, p. 20.

[17] Governments of Canada, the United Mexican States, and the United States of America, Description of the Proposed North American Free Trade Agreement, August 12, 1992.

[18] Congressional Quarterly Almanac 1993, pp. 171-175, 180-181.

[19] A duty drawback is the refund or waiver in whole or in part of customs duties assessed or collected upon importation of an article or materials which are subsequently exported.

[20] Marketing orders were designed to set national guidelines for product quality, market promotion, and supply levels. The most significant Mexican products that were affected by U.S. marketing orders included tomatoes, onions, avocados, grapefruit, oranges, olives, and table grapes.

[21] NAFTA rules of origin for textiles and apparel define when imported textile or apparel goods qualify for preferential treatments. For most products, the rule of origin is "yarn forward", which means that goods must be produced from yarn made in a NAFTA country to benefit from preferential treatment.

[22] Business Roundtable, NAFTA: A Decade of Growth, Prepared by The Trade Partnership, Washington, DC, February 2004, p. 33.

[23] Ibid., p. 30.

[24] Governments of Canada, the United Mexican States, and the United States of America, Description of the Proposed North American Free Trade Agreement, August 12, 1992, p. 12.

[25] Tariff-rate quotas (TRQs) allowed NAFTA partners to export specified quantities of a product to other NAFTA countries at a relatively low tariff, but subjected all imports of the product above a pre-determined threshold to a higher tariff.

[26] Business Roundtable, NAFTA: A Decade of Growth, p. 35.

[27] The Governments of Canada, the United Mexican States, and the United States of America, Description of the Proposed North American Free Trade Agreement, August 12, 1992, pp. 23-24.

[28] United States General Accounting Office (GAO), "North American Free Trade Agreement: Assessment of Major Issues, Volume 2," Report to the Congress, September 1993, pp. 35-36.

[29] Hufbauer and Schott, NAFTA Revisited, pp. 25-29.

[30] GAO, Report to Congress, September 1993, pp. 38-39.

[31] Description of the Proposed North American Free Trade Agreement, August 12, 1992, p. 29.

[32] Description of the Proposed North American Free Trade Agreement, August 12, 1992, pp. 30-31.

[33] Ibid., pp. 31-32.

[34] If the parties are unable to resolve the issue through consultations, they may take the dispute to the NAFTA Trade Commission, which is comprised of Ministers or cabinet-level officers designated by each country. A party may also request the establishment of an arbitral panel, which may make recommendations for the resolution of the dispute.

[35] GAO, Report to Congress, September 1993, pp. 69-71.

[36] The USCAIP, administered by the North American Development Bank, provides financial assistance to communities with significant job losses due to changes in trade patterns with Mexico or Canada as a result of NAFTA.

[37] For more information, see CRS Report RS22823, Overview of Labor Enforcement Issues in Free Trade Agreements, by Mary Jane Bolle, and CRS Report 97-291, NAFTA: Related Environmental Issues and Initiatives, by Mary Tiemann.

[38] Woodrow Wilson International Center for Scholars, NAFTA at 10: Progress, Potential, and Precedents, pp. 20-30.

[39] The Agreement Between the Government of the United States of America and the Government of the United Mexican States Concerning the Establishment of a Border Environment Cooperation Commission and a North American Development Bank, November 1993.

[40] Border Environment Cooperation Commission, 2011 Annual Report, p. 7.

[41] Ibid.

[42] See Ross Perot with Pat Choate, Save Your Job, Save Our Country: Why NAFTA Must be Stopped-Now!, New York, 1993.

[43] For more information, see CRS Report R41660, U.S.-South Korea Free Trade Agreement and Potential Employment Effects: Analysis of Studies, by Mary Jane Bolle and James K. Jackson.

[44] See for example, Gary Clyde Hufbauer and Jeffrey J. Schott, NAFTA Revisited: Achievements and Challenges, Institute for International Economics, October 2005; Center for Strategic and International Studies, NAFTA's Impact on North America: The First Decade, Edited by Sidney Weintraub, 2004; and U.S. Chamber of Commerce, Opening Markets, Creating Jobs: Estimated U.S. Employment Effects of Trade with FTA Partners, 2010.

[45] See for example, Robert E. Scott, Heading South: U.S.-Mexico Trade and Job Displacement under NAFTA, Economic Policy Institute, May 3, 2011; and The Frederick S. Pardee Center, The Future of North American Trade Policy: Lessons from NAFTA, Boston University, November 2009.

[46] Trade statistics in this paragraph are derived from data from the U.S. International Trade Commission's Interactive Tariff and Trade Data Web, at http://dataweb.usitc.gov.

[47] This statistic is based on the Harmonized Tariff Schedule of the United States (HTS). The HTS comprises a hierarchical structure for describing all goods in trade for duty, quota, and statistical purposes. This structure is based upon the international Harmonized Commodity Description and Coding System (HS), administered by the World Customs Organization in Brussels.

[48] Trade statistics in this paragraph are derived from data from the U.S. International Trade Commission's Interactive Tariff and Trade Data Web, at http://dataweb.usitc.gov.

[49] Merchandise trade statistics in this paragraph are derived from data from the U.S. International Trade Commission's Interactive Tariff and Trade Data Web, at http://dataweb.usitc.gov.

[50] Services trade statistics in this paragraph are derived from the Bureau of Economic Analysis online database at http://www.bea.gov.

[51] Congressional Budget Office of the United States, "The Effects of NAFTA on U.S.-Mexican Trade and GDP," A CBO Paper, May 2003, p. xiv.

[52] USITC, "The Impact of Trade Agreements: Effect of the Tokyo Round, U.S.-Israel FTA, U.S.-Canada FTA, NAFTA, and the Uruguay Round on the U.S. Economy," Publication 3621, August 2003.

[53] USITC, "The Impact of the North American Free Trade Agreement on the U.S. Economy and Industries: A Three-Year Review," Publication 3045, June 1997.

[54] Ibid.

[55] Hufbauer and Schott, NAFTA Revisited, pp. 20-21.

[56] Ibid., p. 21.

[57] Lorenzo Caliendo and Fernando Parro, Estimates of the Trade and Welfare Effects of NAFTA, National Bureau of Economic Research, November 2012, pp. 1-5.

[58] Gordon H. Hanson, North American Economic Integration and Industry Location, National Bureau of Economic Research, June 1998.

[60] Business Roundtable, NAFTA: A Decade of Growth, p. 8.

[61] Merchandise trade statistics in this paragraph are derived from data from the U.S. International Trade Commission's Interactive Tariff and Trade Data Web, at http://dataweb.usitc.gov.

[62] See for example, Robert A. Blecker and Gerardo Esquivel, NAFTA, Trade, and Development, Center for U.S.- Mexican Studies (San Diego), El Colegio de la Frontera Norte, Woodrow Wilson International Center for Scholars, and El Colegio de Mexico, WP 10-03, 2010; and Daniel Lederman, William F. Maloney, and Luis Servén, Lessons from NAFTA for Latin America and the Caribbean, The World Bank, 2005.

[63] Rafael E. de Hoyos and Leonardo Iacovone, Economic Performance under NAFTA, The World Bank Development Research Group, May 2011, pp. 25-27.

[64] Daniel Lederman, William F. Maloney, and Luis Servén, Lessons from NAFTA for Latin America and the Caribbean, The World Bank, 2005.

[65] Robert A. Blecker and Gerardo Esquivel, NAFTA, Trade, and Development, Center for U.S.- Mexican Studies, the Mexico Institute of the Woodrow Wilson Center, El Colegio de la Frontera Norte, and El Colegio de México, USMEX WP 10-03, 2010.

[66] Ibid., p. 22.

[67] Robert E. Scott, Carlos Salas, Bruce Campbell and Jeff Faux, Revisiting NAFTA: Still Not Working for North America's Workers, Economic Policy Institute, Briefing Paper #173, p. 43.

[68] Mexico's unilateral agricultural reform measures removed government subsidies and price controls in the agricultural sector that resulted in rising prices for tortillas. Tortillas are the basic staple for the Mexican diet and a necessity of the poor. For this reason, higher prices had a greater effect on the poor than on middle- and higher-income Mexicans. Mexico also reformed its Agrarian Law. Lands that had been distributed to ejidos or community rural groups following the 1910 revolution gained the right to privatize. This led to more efficient production processes, especially in Northern states.

[69] Foreign direct investment data in this section is derived from data from the Bureau of Economic Analysis online database at http://www.bea.gov.

[70] Economic convergence can be broadly defined as a narrowing of the disparities in the economic levels and the manufacturing performances of particular countries or their regions. The goal of the theory of economic convergence is to research and analyze the factors influencing the rates of economic growth and real per capita income in countries.

[71] Robert A. Blecker and Gerardo Esquivel, NAFTA, Trade, and Development, Working Paper 10-03, Center for U.S.- Mexican Studies (San Diego), the Mexico Institute of the Woodrow Wilson Center (Washington DC), El Colegio de la Frontera Norte (Tijuana), and El Colegio de México (Mexico City), 2010, p. 2.

[72] Ibid., pp. 19-23.

[73] Lederman, Maloney, and Servén, Lessons from NAFTA for Latin America and the Caribbean, The World Bank, 2005.

[74] Ibid.

[75] William Easterly, Norbert Fiess, and Daniel Lederman, "NAFTA and Convergence in North America: High Expectations, Big Events, Little Time," Economía, Fall 2003.

[76] John Ibbitson, "After 25 Years, Free-Trade Deal with U.S. Has Helped Canada Grow Up," The Globe and Mail, September 29, 2012.

[77] Kevin Lynch, "Canada's Challenge—From Good to Great," Inside Policy, October 2012.

[78] Glen Hodgson, "Canada U.S. Competitiveness, Addressing the Canadian Economic Contradiction," Woodrow Wilson Center, Canada Institute, June 2007; Lynch, ibid.

[79] Investment statistics are from the U.S. Department of Commerce, Bureau of Economic Analysis, and Statistics Canada.

[80] Ibid.

[81] Douglas Porter, "Free Trade at 25: How the FTA Positioned Canada for the 21st Century," Inside Policy, October 2012.

[82] Julián Aguilar, "Twenty Years Later, NAFTA Remains a Source of Tension," The New York Times, December 7, 2012.

[83] The 12 countries involved in the Trans-Pacific Partnership (TPP) negotiations include the United States, Australia, Brunei, Canada, Chile, Japan, Malaysia, Mexico, New Zealand, Peru, Singapore, and Vietnam. For more information on the TPP, see CRS Report R42694, The Trans-Pacific Partnership (TPP) Negotiations and Issues for Congress, coordinated by Ian F. Fergusson.

[84] The White House, Office of the Press Secretary, Fact Sheet: Key Deliverables for the 2014 North American Leaders Summit, February 19, 2014.

[85] The SPP was endorsed by all three countries, but it was not a signed agreement or treaty and contained no legally binding commitments or obligations. Although the SPP built upon the existing trade and economic relationship of the three countries, it was distinct and separate from NAFTA.

[86] See for example, Society for American Sovereignty, at http://www.americansov.org.

[87] Testimony of Eric Farnsworth, Vice President, Council of the Americas, in U.S. Congress, Senate Committee on Foreign Relations, Doing Business in Latin America: Positive Trends but Serious Challenges, 112th Cong., 2nd sess., July 31, 2012, S.Hrg. 112-607 (Washington, DC: GPO, 2012), pp. 30-32.

[88] Christopher E. Wilson, Working Together: Economic Ties Between the United States and Mexico, Woodrow Wilson International Center for Scholars, November 2011, pp. 37-38.

[89] For more information, see CRS Report R41349, U.S.-Mexican Security Cooperation: The Mérida Initiative and Beyond, by Clare Ribando Seelke and Kristin Finklea.

[90] Robert A. Pastor, The North American Idea: A Vision of a Continental Future, Oxford University Press, 2011, pp. 169-172.

[91] Ibid., pp. 167-200.

In: NAFTA at 20
Editor: Marian Weaver
ISBN: 978-1-63482-779-9

Chapter 2

NAFTA AT 20: NORTH AMERICA'S FREE-TRADE AREA AND ITS IMPACT ON AGRICULTURE*

Steven Zahniser, Sahar Angadjivand, Tom Hertz, Lindsay Kuberka and Alexandra Santos

ABSTRACT

This report examines the integration of North America's agricultural and food markets as a result of the North American Free Trade Agreement (NAFTA), implemented in 1994. NAFTA has had a profound effect on many aspects of North American agriculture over the past two decades.

With a few exceptions, intraregional agricultural trade is now completely free of tariff and quota restrictions, and the agricultural sectors of the member countries—Canada, Mexico, and the United States—have become far more integrated, as is evidenced by rising trade in a wider range of agricultural products, substantial levels of cross-border investment, and important changes in consumption and production.

* This is an edited, reformatted and augmented version of a report, WRS-15-01, issued by the U.S. Department of Agriculture, Economic Research Service, February 2015.

The report also examines recent disputes among its constituents and identifies opportunities for further reforms of mutual benefit to the member countries, with particular attention devoted to the NAFTA governments' efforts to seek deeper regional integration through such means as regulatory cooperation and modifying the agreement's rules of origin and broader access to markets in other parts of the world through the negotiation of additional free-trade agreements.

Keywords: North American Free Trade Agreement, NAFTA, Canada-U.S. Free Trade Agreement, CUSTA, Canada, Mexico, United States, trade, investment, sanitary, phytosanitary

INTRODUCTION

More than 20 years have passed since January 1, 1994, when the North American Free Trade Agreement (NAFTA) was first implemented. On that date, NAFTA's member countries—Canada, Mexico, and the United States—started a 14-year process in which they gradually removed thousands of barriers to intraregional trade, including all agricultural products traded between Mexico and the United States and nearly all agricultural products traded between Canada and the United States and between Canada and Mexico. Canada and the United States already had started to implement bilateral trade liberalization in 1989 as part of the Canada-U.S. Free Trade Agreement (CUSTA), which was then subsumed by NAFTA, so the year 2014 may be thought of as both the 20th anniversary of NAFTA and the 25th anniversary of CUSTA.[1]

NAFTA has had a substantial impact on the integration of North America's agricultural markets. Market integration is the extent to which one or more formerly separated markets have combined to form a single market. Integration is visible in increased cross-border flows of goods, services, capital, and labor. Trade in goods consists of not only final consumer products but also intermediate inputs and raw materials, as firms reorganize their activities around regional markets for both inputs and outputs, spurred in part by greater foreign direct investment (FDI).[2] In addition, decision-makers in both the government and the private sector continue to pursue a course of greater institutional and policy cooperation and coordination to encourage further market integration.

Integration of North America's agricultural markets, as fostered by NAFTA, offers many tangible benefits. In general, it enables agricultural producers and consumers in the region to benefit more fully from their relative strengths and to respond more efficiently to changing economic conditions. For producers, it opens new territories for the sale of their output, possibly allowing for the further exploitation of economies of scale; however, it also opens the door to new competition from producers in locations that were formerly isolated by tariff and quota barriers. In addition, the creation of a larger, single market gives producers access to potentially cheaper suppliers of inputs and creates new opportunities for FDI, as firms restructure their vertical and horizontal arrangements.[3]

For consumers, the formation of a unified market provides access to new varieties of food products and off-season supplies of fresh produce. Greater competition along the food supply chain is likely to make food more affordable, thereby expanding consumer purchasing power.

This report examines the extent to which a single market has taken hold in North American agriculture, provides detail on intraregional trade in specific commodity groups, and describes ongoing efforts to advance the sector's market integration and to establish new free-trade agreements (FTAs) with countries outside NAFTA. The assessment of market integration relies on a framework first presented in ERS's 2005 NAFTA report (Zahniser, 2005).[4]

WHAT IS NAFTA?

NAFTA is a comprehensive economic and trade agreement that establishes a free-trade area encompassing Canada, Mexico, and the United States. NAFTA is structured as three separate bilateral agreements, one between Canada and the United States, a second between Mexico and the United States, and a third between Canada and Mexico.

The first accord is CUSTA, which took effect on January 1, 1989, and was subsumed by NAFTA.

The second and third agreements are found in NAFTA itself, which took effect on January 1, 1994.

Tariff elimination for the items addressed by CUSTA concluded on January 1, 1998. CUSTA exempted certain agricultural products from U.S.-Canada trade liberalization: U.S. imports of dairy products, peanuts, peanut butter, cotton, sugar, and sugar-containing products and Canadian imports of dairy products, poultry, eggs, and margarine.

Quotas that once governed bilateral trade in these commodities were redefined as tariff-rate quotas (TRQs)[5] to comply with the Uruguay Round Agreement on Agriculture (URAA), which took effect on January 1, 1995. NAFTA also exempted dairy and poultry products from Canada-Mexico trade liberalization. Canada has been extremely reluctant to consider full trade liberalization of its dairy, poultry, and egg product sectors, which are governed by supply management and protected by high over-quota tariffs—a long-standing position by Canada in international trade negotiations.[6]

Tariff elimination for the agricultural products addressed by NAFTA concluded on January 1, 2008. NAFTA did not exclude any agricultural products from U.S.-Mexico trade liberalization. Numerous restrictions on bilateral agricultural trade were eliminated immediately upon NAFTA's implementation, while others were phased out over periods of 4, 9, or 14 years. Trade restrictions on the last handful of agricultural commodities (such as U.S. exports to Mexico of corn, dry edible beans, and nonfat dry milk and Mexican exports to the United States of sugar, cucumbers, orange juice, and sprouting broccoli) were removed in 2008. Similar but not identical restrictions on Canada-Mexico trade also were removed at that time.[7]

NAFTA covers much more than tariffs and quotas. The agreement recognizes the right of each member country "to adopt, maintain or apply any sanitary or phytosanitary measure necessary for the protection of human, animal or plant life or health in its territory," and like the URAA, NAFTA requires that sanitary and phytosanitary (SPS) measures be scientifically based, nondiscriminatory, and transparent, and that these measures restrict trade in a minimal fashion. NAFTA also established the NAFTA Committee on Sanitary and Phytosanitary Measures to facilitate technical cooperation between the NAFTA countries in developing, applying, and enforcing SPS measures.

To fulfill these responsibilities, the NAFTA governments have worked to fine tune their SPS measures in ways that facilitate trade and to cooperate on regulatory issues involving trade. Such regulatory cooperation often occurs on a bilateral basis, although the NAFTA Committee on Sanitary and Phytosanitary Measures still meets in response to a direct request from any NAFTA government.

Another important element within NAFTA is the establishment of key principles regarding the treatment of foreign investors. These principles include a firm commitment from each NAFTA country to treat foreign investors from the other member countries no less favorably than it treats its own domestic investors.

In addition, the accord prohibits the application of certain performance requirements on foreign investors, such as a minimum amount of domestic content in production. These provisions reinforce similar changes that Mexico made to its foreign investment laws prior to NAFTA.

NAFTA also created formal mechanisms for the resolution of disputes concerning the agreement's provisions for investment (Chapter 11) and services (Chapter 14), the final antidumping and countervailing duty determinations of the member countries (Chapter 19), and the general interpretation and application of the agreement (Chapter 20). These mechanisms have provided the framework for addressing disputes on a variety of topics, including U.S. countervailing duties (CVDs) on live swine from Canada, Mexican antidumping duties (ADs) on selected U.S. apples, Mexico's former sales tax on beverages made from sweeteners other than cane sugar, NAFTA's provisions for cross-border trucking between Mexico and the United States, and Canada's application of TRQs allowed under the URAA to U.S. products imported under NAFTA. As of October 2014, the NAFTA Secretariat (2014) listed just one active dispute settlement case under Chapters 19 or 20 of NAFTA that directly concerns agricultural products—an AD case involving Mexican imports of U.S. chicken thighs and legs—and the duties in this case have been suspended by the Mexican Government so that Mexico's poultry market can stabilize following outbreaks of Highly Pathogenic Avian Influenza (HPAI) in several poultry-producing areas in that country.

Antidumping duties are currently in effect for just a handful of agricultural products traded among the NAFTA countries: Canadian imports of refined sugar in granulated, liquid, and powdered form and whole potatoes from the United States; U.S. imports of citric acid and certain citrate salts from Canada; and Mexican imports of epoxidized soybean oil from the United States (Canada Border Services Agency, 2014; México, Secretaría de Economía, Unidad de Prácticas Comerciales Internacionales, 2014; U.S. International Trade Commission, 2014a). No CVDs are currently in effect with respect to intraregional agricultural trade. Over the past several years, however, two major developments occurred in the AD/CVD arena: in March 2013, a new agreement suspending a U.S. antidumping investigation of tomato imports from Mexico took effect, and in October 2014, draft agreements were completed to suspend U.S. AD and CVD investigations regarding sugar imports from Mexico. These developments are discussed later in the report.

Table 1. NAFTA has advanced the integration of many aspects of North American agriculture

	General comments	U.S.-Mexico	U.S.-Canada
Grains and oilseeds	Sizable increases in U.S. exports to Mexico and Canadian exports to the United States and Mexico. Important cross-border investments in grain milling. Expanded biofuel production increases demand for certain grains and oilseeds.	***Pre-1994:*** *Low degree of integration.* Mexico tightly regulated importation of corn, wheat, and barley via import permits. Sorghum, with duty-free access to the Mexican market, rivaled corn as the leading feed grain imported by Mexico. ***Now:*** *High degree of integration.* Corn emerges as leading feed commodity imported by Mexico. Strong linkages between U.S. grain and oilseed farmers and Mexican livestock producers. Mexican direct investment is present in the U.S. baking and tortilla industries.	***Pre-1989:*** *Medium degree of integration.* Tariffs and other trade-related policies discourage North-South trade in wheat and wheat products. Moderate tariffs impeded bilateral trade in vegetable oils. ***Now:*** *High degree of integration.* Growing two-way trade encompasses bulk commodities, feed ingredients, and processed foods. Separate from NAFTA, Canada ends single-desk trading authority of Canadian Wheat Board (CWB).
Livestock and animal products	U.S. and Canadian beef exporters regain access to many Asian markets following coordinated response by NAFTA governments to detections of bovine spongiform encephalopathy (BSE) in Canada and United States. Canada and Mexico challenge	***Pre-1994:*** *Medium degree of integration, except Mexican exports of pork and poultry meat (low).* Mexico already supplied substantial number of feeder cattle to United States and had a most- favored-nation (MFN) tariff of zero on beef imports until 1992. ***Now:*** *High degree of integration, except Mexican exports of pork and*	***Pre-1989:*** *Medium degree of integration in cattle, beef, hogs, and pork.* U.S. and Canadian beef quotas discouraged integration of cattle and beef sectors. Two-way trade in beef and U.S. imports of Canadian pork already underway. *Low degree of integration in dairy, poultry, and egg products due to*

	General comments	U.S.-Mexico	U.S.-Canada
	U.S. requirements for mandatory country-of-origin labeling (COOL) at WTO. With the removal of tariffs and quotas (except for supply managed commodities in Canada), progress in addressing the sanitary concerns of importing countries becomes crucial to further market integration.	*poultry meat (low).* U.S. meat exports to Mexico double in volume during NAFTA period. Largest chicken producer in Mexico owns hatchery in United States; second largest is an affiliate of a Brazilian firm with operations that formerly belonged to U.S. firms. Mexican beef exports to U.S. and Asian markets increase. U.S. imports of Mexican pork and poultry meat remain low due to sanitary concerns.	*supply management.* ***Now:*** *High degree of integration in cattle, beef, hogs, and pork.* Expanded Canadian hog exports to U.S. include larger proportion of feeder animals that are finished in the United States. Sizable levels of two-way trade in beef and cattle. *Low degree of integration in dairy, poultry, and egg products.* Supply management continues. Canadian re-export programs allow some imports of U.S. product, but only if used as inputs in manufacture of processed foods for export.
Fruit and vegetables	Attention to food safety and coordination of phytosanitary measures are central to integration. Trade expansion is related to increased consumption of fresh produce, particularly in Canada and the United States, on both seasonal and aggregate levels. Search for risk-mitigating tools for intraregional produce trade continues despite creation	***Pre-1994:*** *Medium degree of integration for most commodities.* Many U.S. tariffs were designed on a seasonal basis to protect U.S. produce as it entered the market. Phytosanitary protocols did not yet exist to facilitate U.S. imports of fresh avocados from Mexico. ***Now:*** *High degree of integration.* Large volumes of bilateral trade. Mexico surpasses Canada to become	***Pre-1989:*** *Medium degree of integration.* Tariffs limited some aspects of bilateral trade. U.S. produce exports to Canada encompassed multiple commodities, while potatoes accounted for bulk of U.S. produce imports from Canada. ***Now:*** *High degree of integration.* Canadian consumers have duty-free access to full range of U.S.

Table 1. (Continued)

	General comments	U.S.-Mexico	U.S.-Canada
	of Fruit and Vegetable Dispute Resolution Corporation (DRC). In 2014, USDA withdraws special status that Canadian produce exporters previously had enjoyed under Perishable Agricultural Commodities Act (PACA).	largest foreign market for U.S. apples and pears. DRC closes its Mexico office in 2007 due to lack of participation by Mexican buyers.	produce. Canada is now an important supplier of greenhouse tomatoes, cucumbers, and peppers to the United States, in addition to fresh and frozen potatoes.
Sugar and sweeteners	Growing intraregional trade in processed foods containing sweeteners. Such trade may substitute for sugar trade to some extent in case of Canada-U.S. trade. Draft agreements are reached to suspend U.S. antidumping and countervailing duty investigations regarding sugar imports from Mexico. Investigations were launched in 2014 in response to petition filed by U.S. industry groups, following unusually large crops in 2012 and 2013.	***Pre-1994:*** *Low degree of integration:* Negligible bilateral trade in sugar and high-fructose corn syrup (HFCS). Some trade in sweetener-containing products. ***Now:*** *High degree of integration.* Large volumes of U.S. sugar imports from Mexico and U.S. HFCS exports to Mexico. Exchange, analysis, and dissemination of market information by U.S.-Mexico Governmental Sweetener Working Committee. Trade restrictions in draft suspension agreements may have potential to lessen integration of U.S. and Mexican sugar markets.	***Pre-1989:*** *Low degree of integration.* Some bilateral trade in sweetener- containing processed foods, such as confectionery products and baked goods. ***Now:*** *Low degree of integration.* Exemption of U.S. imports from Canada of sugar and sugar-containing products from bilateral trade liberalization. Low levels of bilateral trade in sugar, but growing trade in maple syrup, glucose and glucose syrup, and HFCS.

	General comments	U.S.-Mexico	U.S.-Canada
Cotton, textiles, and apparel	World Trade Organization's Agreement on Textiles and Clothing leads to much greater competition from China, India, Pakistan, Bangladesh, Vietnam, and other non-NAFTA countries.	***Pre-1994:*** *Medium degree of integration.* Bilateral textile and apparel agreement of 1988 broadened quotas in several categories of product. ***Now:*** *High degree of integration.* Specialization in which United States supplies cotton to Mexico and Mexico supplies cotton textiles and apparel to United States continues despite increased imports from non-NAFTA countries.	***Pre-1989:*** *Medium degree of integration.* Trade barriers sustained Canadian textile and apparel output and U.S. cotton exports to Canada. ***Now:*** *High degree of integration.* U.S.-Canada textile and apparel trade continues, but Canada shifts away from importation and milling of cotton.
Processed foods	Long-standing U.S. direct investment in Canadian and Mexican processed food sectors. Sales of Canadian and Mexican affiliates of U.S. processed food companies still exceed U.S. processed food exports to those countries.	***Pre-1994:*** *Low degree of integration.* Tariff barriers helped to keep bilateral processed food trade at low levels. ***Now:*** *High degree of integration.* Substantial U.S. investment in Mexico's food industry, with some Mexican investments in the U.S. food industry. Beer is Mexico's leading agricultural export to the United States.	***Pre-1989:*** *Medium degree of integration.* Tariffs inhibited many aspects of bilateral processed food trade. Baked goods, confectionery products, pet food, and beer were among leading products traded. ***Now:*** *High degree of integration.* Substantial U.S. and Canadian direct investment in each other's processed food industries. Significant and growing intra-industry trade in intermediate and final food products.

Source: USDA, Economic Research Service.

Overview of North American Market Integration

Table 1 presents an overview of changes in the level of market integration in North American agriculture since the implementation of NAFTA, using the framework established in ERS's 2005 NAFTA report (Zahniser, 2005). This framework focuses on two main characteristics of each agricultural subsector: (1) cross-border economic activity—primarily agricultural trade and intra-regional FDI; and (2) the tariffs, quotas, and other barriers in place that limit cross-border trade and investment.[8] Most sectors within North American agriculture now feature a *high* degree of integration, defined by substantial flows of cross-border trade and investment and the removal of most major barriers to trade and investment, in large part due to NAFTA. Because the agreement's process of trade liberalization was so sweeping, very few agricultural sectors are currently marked by a *medium* degree of integration, defined by the presence of one or more significant barriers to trade and/or investment. Recent examples of sectors characterized by a medium degree of integration include the U.S. and Canadian wheat markets prior to the end of the single-desk trading authority of the Canadian Wheat Board (CWB) and the markets adversely affected by the retaliatory tariffs applied by Mexico from March 2009 to October 2011 in conjunction with the U.S.-Mexico trucking dispute, which is now resolved. The degree of market integration is *low* in sectors that were excluded from NAFTA's project of agricultural trade liberalization, such as the U.S. and Canadian dairy, poultry, and egg product sectors. Prior to NAFTA, a number of agricultural sectors, such as the U.S. and Mexican grain and oilseed sectors, had a low degree of market integration due to the presence of substantial tariffs, quotas, and other trade restrictions.

Intraregional Agricultural Trade More than Triples

Agricultural trade among NAFTA's member countries has grown tremendously during the NAFTA period (figure 1).[9] The total value of intraregional agricultural trade (exports and imports) among all three NAFTA countries reached about $82.0 billion in 2013, compared with $16.7 billion in 1993 (the year before NAFTA's implementation) and $8.8 billion in 1988 (the year before CUSTA's implementation).[10]

When the effects of inflation are taken into account, this expansion in intraregional agricultural trade corresponds to an increase of 233 percent between 1993 and 2013. Over the same period, increases of this proportion or larger are also present in the volumes of many agricultural commodities traded among the NAFTA countries (app. tables 1-4).

TRADE LIBERALIZATION ALSO SPURS AGRICULTURAL TRADE BETWEEN THE NAFTA COUNTRIES AND THE REST OF THE WORLD

Overall, intraregional agricultural trade among the NAFTA countries grew at a faster pace during the past two decades than agricultural trade between the NAFTA countries and the rest of the world. Between 1991-93 and 2010-12, intraregional agricultural trade (as reflected in export data) expanded at a compound annual rate of 7.9 percent, while agricultural trade with the rest of the world (exports and imports combined) increased at a rate of 6.9 percent. An analysis of agricultural trade shares conducted by Zahniser and Herrera Moreno (2014) and reproduced in the table underscores the importance of additional trade agreements negotiated by the NAFTA countries with countries in other parts of the world subsequent to NAFTA to the growth of North American agricultural trade with the rest of the world.[1]

For instance, Mexico's free-trade agreements (FTAs) in addition to NAFTA have broadened the customer base for Mexican agricultural products to encompass both middle-income economies in Central and South America and the upper income economies of Europe and Japan. As a result, Mexico's FTA partners outside NAFTA purchased 13.6 percent of Mexico's total agricultural exports during 2010-12, compared with 7.0 percent during 1991-93. Similarly, China and Hong Kong's combined share of total U.S. agricultural exports climbed from 3.3 to 18.3 percent between 1991-93 and 2010-12, and their share of total Canadian agricultural exports increased from 7.2 to 10.2 percent, due to China's accession to the WTO and the general opening of China to the global economy.

Agricultural trade of the NAFTA countries by trade partner: Annual averages and shares, 1991-93 versus 2010-12

NAFTA	NAFTA partners		Other FTA partners		China and Hong Kong		Rest of world		Total	
	1991-93	2010-12	1991-93	2010-12	1991-93	2010-12	1991-93	2010-12	1991-93	2010-12
	Values in billions of U.S. dollars (shares in percent in parentheses)									
Exports by:										
U.S.	8.4	36.1	4.6	16.4	1.4	23.9	27.4	54.6	41.9	131.2
	(20.1)	(27.6)	(11.0)	(12.5)	(3.3)	(18.3)	(65.5)	(41.7)	(100)	(100)
Mexico	3.3	17.0	0.3	2.9	0.0	0.3	0.1	0.9	3.7	21.0
	(88.9)	(81.0)	(7.0)	(13.6)	(0.2)	(1.3)	(3.9)	(4.1)	(100)	(100)
Canada	6.2	23.4	0.2	0.9	0.8	4.5	4.5	14.8	11.7	43.6
	(52.6)	(53.7)	(1.8)	(2.1)	(7.2)	(10.2)	(38.4)	(34.0)	(100)	(100)
Imports by:										
U.S.	6.6	33.7	4.4	14.1	0.5	4.0	12.7	42.7	24.3	94.6
	(27.1)	(35.7)	(18.3)	(15.0)	(2.1)	(4.3)	(52.5)	(45.1)	(100)	(100)
Mexico	4.0	20.4	0.8	2.8	0.0	0.4	0.6	1.8	5.4	25.5
	(72.8)	(80.0)	(15.0)	(11.2)	(0.4)	(1.6)	(11.8)	(7.2)	(100)	(100)
Canada	5.0	20.6	0.4	1.8	0.2	1.1	2.7	9.7	8.3	33.2
	(60.6)	(62.1)	(4.6)	(5.5)	(2.0)	(3.3)	(32.8)	(29.2)	(100)	(100)

Note: Canada's trade statistics cover both agri-food and seafood products. "Other FTA partners" are defined as a given country's FTA partners outside of NAFTA, as of September 2014. Thus, the sets of countries listed in the table as "FTA countries" and "Rest of world" in the columns for 1991-93 are the same as for 2010-12. Percentages within rows may not sum to 100 percent due to rounding.

Source: Reproduction of table 2 in Zahniser and Herrera Moreno (2014). Canadian and U.S. data were obtained from Statistics Canada, as cited by Agriculture and Agri-Food Canada (2013), and USDA/FAS (2014a), respectively. Mexican data were obtained directly from México, Secretaría de Economía. Nominal annual exchange rates from U.S. Department of Agriculture, Economic Research Service (2014b) were used to convert Canadian trade statistics to U.S. dollars.

[1]Table 8 provides a full list of the NAFTA countries' FTAs other than NAFTA.

U.S. agricultural exports to the NAFTA countries continue to grow, both at the aggregate level and at the commodity level for many products. When this trade is measured in quantity rather than value, however, U.S. exports to Canada and Mexico of certain bulk agricultural commodities have slowed over the past decade. Corn exports to Mexico have fluctuated greatly since 2008, without exhibiting a clear upward or downward trend, while sorghum and soybean exports to Mexico and corn and soybean exports to Canada have been on the decline for more than a decade (figure 2).[11] Factors behind these developments include periods of drought that adversely affected crop and livestock production in multiple regions of the United States over the past 5 years; increased Canadian production of corn, rapeseed, and soybeans; competing buyers for agricultural commodities in countries outside NAFTA; the use of large quantities of U.S.-grown corn as an ethanol feedstock; expanded exports of distillers dried grains with solubles (DDGS), a co-product of corn-based ethanol production that is used as an animal feed; and a partial shift by Mexican livestock producers from sorghum to corn, especially since the initiation of duty-free U.S. corn exports to Mexico as part of NAFTA in 2008.

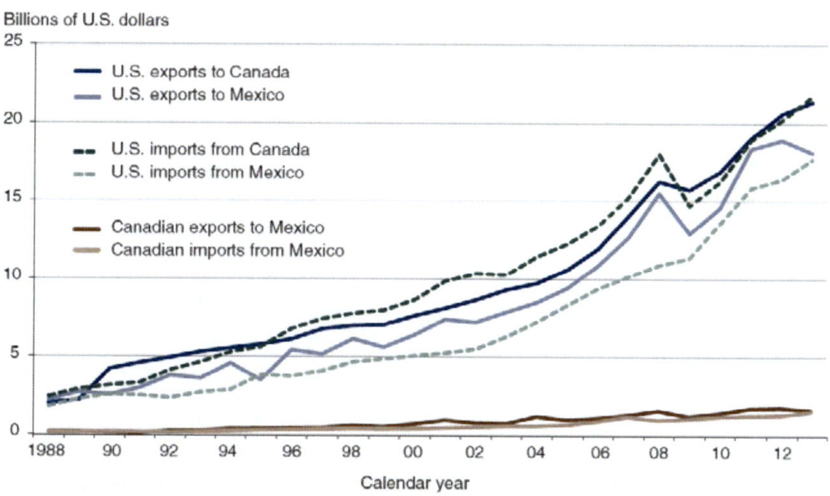

CUSTA= Canada-U.S. Free Trade Agreement. NAFTA = North American Free Trade Agreement.

Source: USDA, Economic Research Service, using U.S. trade data from U.S. Department of Commerce, Bureau of the Census, *Foreign Trade Statistics*, as presented by USDA/FAS (2014a), and Canadian trade data (for Canada-Mexico trade) from Statistics Canada, CATSNET Analytics (2014).

Figure 1. Intraregional agricultural trade has experienced tremendous growth during the CUSTA-NAFTA period.

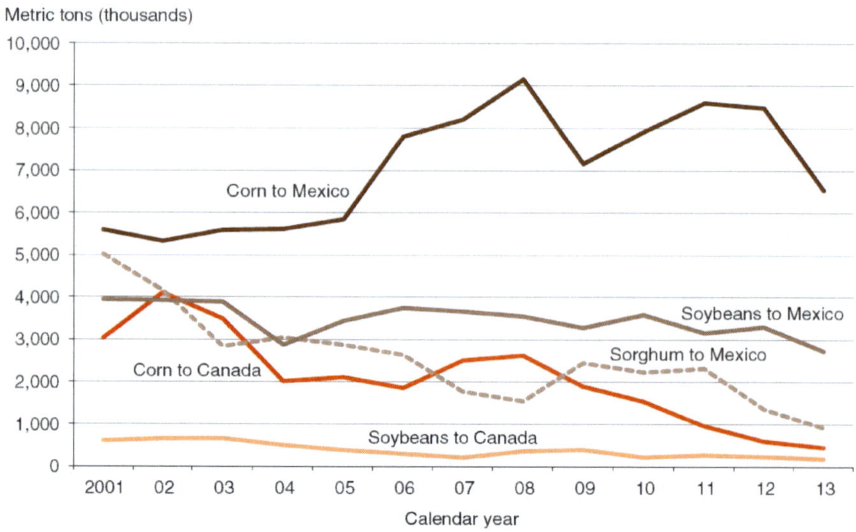

NAFTA = North American Free Trade Agreement.

Source: USDA, Economic Research Service, using data from U.S. Department of Commerce, Bureau of the Census, *Foreign Trade Statistics*, as presented by USDA/FAS (2014a).

Figure 2. U.S. exports to the NAFTA countries have slowed over the past decade for some bulk agricultural commodities.

Different methodologies used by researchers to evaluate NAFTA's trade effects generate different estimates. Results of a computable general equilibrium (CGE) model presented in ERS's 1997 NAFTA Report (Crawford and Link, 1997), for example, indicate that U.S. agricultural exports to Canada and Mexico during 1994-96 were about 7 percent and 3 percent higher, respectively, than they would have been had the agreement not been in place, while U.S. agricultural imports from Canada and Mexico were about 5 percent and 3 percent higher, respectively. Results from a CGE model that considered the potential effects of Mexico's withdrawal from NAFTA and the resulting loss of Mexico's preferential access to the U.S. and Canadian markets (Zahniser and Burfisher, 2007) suggest that Mexico's agricultural exports (to all countries) would fall by 7 percent, compared with a 2001 base, while corresponding imports would decline by 18 percent.

A number of researchers have estimated NAFTA's impact on agricultural trade using gravity models, in which the level of trade between two economies is posited to be positively related to their size and negatively related to any impediments to bilateral trade. In a study of the effects of FTAs on international trade in chicken, beef, and pork during the period 2001-05, Ghazalian et al. (2011) conclude that meat trade among the NAFTA countries has benefited both from the removal of tariffs and quotas and from progress in the area of nontariff measures (NTMs). In particular, the authors estimate that the effects on intraregional meat trade of removing tariffs and quotas—increases of 49 percent for chicken, 48 percent for beef, and 5 percent for pork—are smaller than the effects of nontariff preferences among the NAFTA countries—121 percent for chicken, 216 percent for beef, and 163 percent for pork. In a study of agricultural and food trade during the years 1995, 2000, and 2004, Lambert and McKoy (2009) associate membership in NAFTA with higher levels of trade in agricultural products in 1995 and 2000 and in food products in 2000 and 2004. In a study covering the period 1985-2000, Jayasinghe and Sarker (2008) find the presence of a positive "NAFTA bloc effect" on the order of 100-300 percent for vegetable trade and over 1,000 percent for red meat, meaning that bilateral trade in these products is estimated to be that much larger when occurring between two NAFTA countries.

ERS assessments in the 2002 NAFTA report (Zahniser and Link, 2002) emphasize that the agreement's trade effects vary by commodity and trade partner, with the biggest changes in trade occurring in the commodities that underwent the most significant reductions in tariff and nontariff barriers. In that analysis, which focused on trade developments between 1994 and 2000, NAFTA was found to have had a large positive impact (15 percent or more) on the following components of U.S. agricultural trade, relative to what would have occurred in the absence of NAFTA: exports to Canada of wheat products, beef and veal, and cotton; exports to Mexico of rice, cattle and calves, nonfat dry milk, cotton, processed potatoes, apples, and pears; imports from Canada of wheat, wheat products, and beef and veal; and imports from Mexico of wheat products, peanuts, and sugar.

Retaliatory Tariffs Imposed during NAFTA Trucking Dispute Reveal Importance of Duty-Free Access

What would happen if the preferential market access secured by NAFTA were lost? Some U.S. exporters and their Mexican customers had this very experience from March 19, 2009, to October 20, 2011, when the Mexican Government imposed retaliatory tariffs on selected agricultural and nonagricultural products from the United States. These tariffs, which generally corresponded to Mexico's most-favored-nation (MFN) tariffs, were imposed in association with a dispute that has since been resolved concerning NAFTA's provisions for cross-border, long-haul trucking between Mexico and the United States and in accordance with NAFTA's dispute-resolution procedures.

The retaliatory tariffs were imposed in March 2009 following the cancellation of a U.S. demonstration project for NAFTA's trucking provisions. NAFTA's dispute-resolution procedure allowed the Mexican Government to suspend U.S. trade benefits of "equivalent effect" to the trucking provisions until the two countries settled the dispute. In February 2001, the Mexican Government won a decision regarding the dispute at a NAFTA arbitration panel, following President Clinton's decision in December 1995 to postpone implementation of the agreement's trucking provisions (NAFTA Arbitral Panel, 2001: p. 83). This panel decision thereby gave Mexico the option to retaliate should the issue not be resolved. In October 2011, the United States launched a new demonstration project, and duty-free trade once again resumed for the products subject to the retaliatory tariffs.

Table 2 contrasts the average annual level of Mexican agricultural imports from the United States targeted by the retaliatory tariffs during the tariff period (roughly March 2009 to October 2011) with their average annual level during a comparison period encompassing months just prior to the tariffs' imposition and just after their removal (March 2006 to February 2009 and November 2011 to October 2013). The table does not include the nonagricultural imports subject to these tariffs. As shown in the table, 46 of the 53 targeted agricultural imports declined in value during the tariff period.

By adding the percentage increase in Mexican agricultural imports from the United States not covered by the retaliatory tariffs (2.3 percent) to the percentage decline in imports covered by the tariffs (19.1 percent), one can obtain a rough estimate of the retaliatory tariffs' impact. Compared with the level during the comparison period, the tariffs reduced the total value of the targeted U.S. agricultural exports to Mexico during this period by an estimated 21.4 percent, or a total of about $1.1 billion when the entire 32-month tariff period is taken into account. Because we compare the change in agricultural imports covered by the tariffs with the change in agricultural imports not covered by the tariffs, this calculation provides a simple control for the trade effects of the global economic downturn that started in late 2007, since both groups of imports were influenced by the recession.

Table 2. Retaliatory tariffs associated with the U.S.-Mexico trucking dispute had a pronounced effect on Mexican agricultural imports from the United State

Mexican agricultural imports from the United States		Annual averages								
		Value			Volume			Unit value		
Mexico's HS code	**Product**	**Comparison period**	**Tariff period**	**Change**	**Comparison period**	**Tariff period**	**Change**	**Comparison period**	**Tariff period**	**Change**
		Millions of dollars		*Percent*	*Metric tons*		*Percent*	*Dollars per kilogram*		*Percent*
	Total	15,314.39	15,263.16	-0.3	--	--	--	--	--	--
	Not subject to retaliatory tariffs	13,415.34	13,727.71	2.3	--	--	--	--	--	--
	Subject to retaliatory tariffs	1,899.05	1,535.45	-19.1	--	--	--	--	--	--
02031201	Meat of swine, legs, ham, and cuts thereof, bone-in, fresh or chilled[2]	458.06	559.14	22.1	267,085	288,151	7.9	1.72	1.94	13.1
02032201	Meat of swine, legs, ham, and cuts thereof, bone-in, frozen[2]	13.91	3.76	-73.0	6,958	1,743	-75.0	2.00	2.16	7.9
04061001	Fresh cheese (unripened or uncured), including that from whey cheese, and curd[2]	47.70	19.37	-59.4	12,971	4,947	-61.9	3.68	3.92	6.5

Table 2. (Continued)

Mexican agricultural imports from the United States		Annual averages								
		Value			Volume			Unit value		
Mexico's HS code	Product	Comparison period	Tariff period	Change	Comparison period	Tariff period	Change	Comparison period	Tariff period	Change
04063099	Processed cheese, not grated or powdered[2]	1.35	1.46	7.7	290	421	45.1	4.67	3.46	-25.8
04069004 & 04069099	Cheese, not elsewhere specified or indicated[2]	112.02	76.72	-31.5	25,541	17,157	-32.8	4.39	4.47	2.0
06049102 & 06049003	Christmas trees, fresh	15.04	9.28	-38.3	19,033	16,160	-15.1	0.79	0.57	-27.3
07031001	Onions	29.90	12.98	-56.6	64,239	46,015	-28.4	0.47	0.28	-39.4
07051101	Iceberg lettuce	17.28	6.57	-62.0	40,594	23,106	-43.1	0.43	0.28	-33.2
07104001	Sweet corn, frozen[2]	8.57	6.84	-20.2	7,492	7,453	-0.5	1.14	0.92	-19.8
08021201	Almonds, shelled	39.06	23.57	-39.7	6,643	6,585	-0.9	5.88	3.58	-39.1
08025001, 08025099, 08025101, & 08025201	Pistachios, fresh or dried[2]	6.65	5.28	-20.7	1,000	907	-9.3	6.65	5.82	-12.5
08041001	Dates, fresh	0.33	0.26	-22.0	231	198	-14.2	1.43	1.30	-9.1
08041099	Dates, other	0.47	0.25	-47.4	115	63	-45.4	4.11	3.96	-3.6
08051001	Oranges, fresh or dried[2]	7.70	4.85	-37.0	25,350	24,147	-4.7	0.30	0.20	-33.9

Mexican agricultural imports from the United States		Annual averages								
		Value			Volume			Unit value		
Mexico's HS code	Product	Comparison period	Tariff period	Change	Comparison period	Tariff period	Change	Comparison period	Tariff period	Change
08054001	Grapefruit or pomelos, fresh or dried[2]	1.17	0.46	-61.0	7,435	2,374	-68.1	0.16	0.19	22.1
08061001	Grapes, fresh	73.89	29.80	-59.7	49,898	32,529	-34.8	1.48	0.92	-38.1
08081001	Apples, fresh[2]	244.61	178.31	-27.1	204,161	173,019	-15.3	1.20	1.03	-14.0
08082001 & 08083001	Pears, fresh	81.25	52.32	-35.6	77,594	69,498	-10.4	1.05	0.75	-28.1
08091001	Apricots, fresh[2]	2.74	1.01	-63.0	1,645	964	-41.4	1.67	1.05	-36.9
08092001, 08092101, & 08092901	Cherries, fresh[2]	3.61	2.68	-25.7	912	546	-40.1	3.96	4.91	24.1
08101001	Strawberries, fresh	26.07	14.35	-45.0	18,590	14,580	-21.6	1.40	0.98	-29.8
08133001	Apples, dried[2]	1.90	1.66	-12.4	288	238	-17.1	6.61	6.99	5.7
08135001	Mixtures of dried fruit or nuts	6.17	5.45	-11.6	1,027	939	-8.5	6.01	5.80	-3.4
11041201	Oats, rolled or flaked[2]	5.96	8.47	42.0	7,823	10,536	34.7	0.76	0.80	5.4
16024901	Swine meat, prepared[2]	15.29	12.29	-19.6	4,288	3,725	-13.1	3.56	3.30	-7.5
17041001	Chewing gum, including those coated in sugar[2]	3.24	6.74	107.7	661	1,068	61.5	4.91	6.31	28.6
18063101	Chocolate, filled[2]	25.15	13.55	-46.1	6,627	3,045	-54.1	3.79	4.45	17.3
18063201	Chocolate, not filled[2]	16.29	9.76	-40.1	3,374	2,068	-38.7	4.83	4.72	-2.3

Table 2. (Continued)

Mexican agricultural imports from the United States		Annual averages								
		Value			Volume			Unit value		
Mexico's HS code	Product	Comparison period	Tariff period	Change	Comparison period	Tariff period	Change	Comparison period	Tariff period	Change
19021999	Pasta, not containing egg, not cooked, filled, or otherwise prepared	5.89	7.68	30.5	2,463	3,038	23.4	2.39	2.53	5.8
20041001	Potatoes, frozen	82.93	42.67	-48.5	79,799	42,894	-46.2	1.04	0.99	-4.3
20054001	Peas, prepared or preserved, except in vinegar or acetic acid, not frozen	0.34	0.24	-29.2	263	167	-36.6	1.30	1.45	11.8
20081101	Peanuts, shelled	7.06	6.83	-3.2	3,046	3,422	12.3	2.32	2.00	-13.8
20081199	Peanuts, with shell	4.29	3.49	-18.5	1,443	1,374	-4.8	2.97	2.54	-14.4
20081901	Almonds, prepared or preserved	4.52	3.95	-12.6	580	680	17.2	7.79	5.81	-25.4
20081999	Mixed nuts, prepared or preserved	59.93	38.83	-35.2	20,462	10,659	-47.9	2.93	3.64	24.4
20086001	Cherries, prepared or preserved	6.68	3.73	-44.2	2,515	1,487	-40.9	2.65	2.51	-5.6
20098001, 20098101, & 20098999	Fruit or vegetable juice, other than orange, grapefruit, other citric fruit, lime, pineapple, tomato, grape, or apple[1]	7.90	7.61	-3.7	2,833	2,009	-29.1	2.79	3.79	35.7
20099001	Mixtures of vegetable juice only[1]	0.31	0.30	-0.7	114	106	-6.3	2.69	2.85	6.0

Mexican agricultural imports from the United States		Annual averages								
		Value			Volume			Unit value		
Mexico's HS code	Product	Comparison period	Tariff period	Change	Comparison period	Tariff period	Change	Comparison period	Tariff period	Change
20099099	Mixtures of fruit or vegetable juice, other than mixtures of vegetable juice only[1]	9.50	8.75	-8.0	3,378	2,781	-17.7	2.81	3.14	11.8
21031001	Soy sauce	6.11	5.60	-8.4	4,579	4,074	-11.0	1.33	1.37	3.0
21032001	Ketchup[2]	11.79	11.25	-4.5	10,386	10,117	-2.6	1.13	1.11	-2.0
21039099	Condiments, other than soy sauce, ketchup and other tomato sacues, mustard meal, and pre-pared mustard	119.18	102.50	-14.0	56,861	50,534	-11.1	2.10	2.03	-3.2
21041001	Prepared pottages, soups, and broths, and preparations for such foods	184.97	144.86	-21.7	50,851	43,861	-13.7	3.64	3.30	-9.2
21069006	Concentrates of juice from a single fruit or vegetable, enriched with vitamins or minerals	0.38	0.22	-41.3	223	121	-45.8	1.72	1.86	8.3
21069007	Concentrates of juice from more than one fruit or vegetable, enriched with vitamins or minerals	1.13	0.59	-47.6	332	274	-17.5	3.41	2.16	-36.5

Table 2. (Continued)

Mexican agricultural imports from the United States		Annual averages								
		Value			Volume			Unit value		
Mexico's HS code	Product	Comparison period	Tariff period	Change	Comparison period	Tariff period	Change	Comparison period	Tariff period	Change
21069008	Food preparations not elsewhere specified or indicated, with a content of milk solids greater than 10 percent in weight	17.66	16.33	-7.6	3,648	4,331	18.7	4.84	3.77	-22.1
22011001	Mineral water[1]	3.09	3.66	18.6	12,665	15,216	20.1	0.24	0.24	-1.3
22041099	Sparkling wine, other than champagne[1]	0.23	0.76	225.8	458	744	62.6	0.51	1.03	100.4
22042102	Red, rose, claret, or white wine, whose alcoholic strength by volume is up to 14 percent at [2]0 degrees Celsius, in containers of clay, ceramics, or glass less than or equal to [2] liters1	6.45	5.13	-20.5	1,682	1,647	-2.1	3.84	3.11	-18.8
22060099	Other fermented beverages or mixtures of fermented and non-alcoholic beverages, not elsewhere specified[1]	11.74	8.06	-31.4	6,588	5,123	-22.2	1.78	1.57	-11.8

Mexican agricultural imports from the United States		Annual averages								
		Value			Volume			Unit value		
Mexico's HS code	Product	Comparison period	Tariff period	Change	Comparison period	Tariff period	Change	Comparison period	Tariff period	Change
23063001	Sunflower seed meal and oilcake	0.54	0.30	-44.2	2,739	1,212	-55.7	0.20	0.25	26.0
23064999	Rape seed meal or oilcake with a high content of erucic acid	0.137	0.001	-99.3	404.01	0.12	-100.0	0.34	8.27	2,334.4
23091001	Dog or cat food, for retail sale	80.91	44.94	-44.5	91,769	34,787	-62.1	0.88	1.29	46.5

Note: Comparison period runs from March 2006 to February 2009 and from November 2011 to October 2013. Unless otherwise indicated, the tariff period used in the analysis runs from March 2009 to October 2011, corresponding with the actual tariff period from March 19, 2009, to October 20, 2011.

[1] Volume measured in thousands of liters and unit value measured in dollars per liter.

[2] Tariff period used in the analysis runs from September 2010 to October 2011, corresponding with the actual tariff period for these commodities from August 19, 2010, to October 20, 2011.

Source: USDA, Economic Research Service, using Mexico, Secretariat of Economy, as cited by Global Trade Information Services, Inc. (2014).

Broader Seasonal Availability of Fresh Produce and Greater Variety of Food Products

In addition to increasing intraregional agricultural trade, NAFTA has helped to broaden the seasonal availability of fresh produce and to increase the variety of food products available to consumers. For instance, trade liberalization makes it easier for North American consumers to access fresh tomatoes throughout the year, given the existence of protected[12] and open-field tomato production in each NAFTA country, which as a group have shipping seasons covering the entire calendar year (Cook and Calvin, 2005). In an analysis of the changing composition of U.S. agricultural imports from Mexico, Jabara and Lynch (2006) find that products not imported by the United States from Mexico in 1993 accounted for about 18 percent of U.S. agricultural imports from Mexico in 2005. Among the "new varieties" of imports identified by Jabara and Lynch are grape tomatoes and fresh avocados—products whose importation has benefited not only from trade liberalization under NAFTA but also from the introduction of a grape tomato variety from Taiwan and more trade- oriented phytosanitary regulations for fresh avocados.

Trade liberalization, trade-oriented phytosanitary standards, and rapid development of the Mexican supermarket sector have given Mexican consumers much wider opportunities to purchase noncitrus fruit such as apples, pears, and grapes from the United States, to the point where Mexico has surpassed Canada to become the leading foreign market for U.S. apples and pears. Similarly, liberalization of U.S.-Canada trade has given Canadians duty-free access to the full range of U.S. produce, facilitating U.S. exports of strawberries, cherries, pears, carrots, lettuce, and potatoes, among other commodities, although all of these products were familiar to Canadian consumers before CUSTA.

A Small, Positive Net Effect on U.S. Agricultural Employment

By opening the door to new export opportunities and allowing for a more efficient allocation of productive resources across economic sectors and geographic areas, NAFTA has increased the opportunities for agricultural employment, particularly in those subsectors of agriculture where the United States enjoys a clear comparative advantage, such as grains and oilseeds. NAFTA's net impact on U.S. agricultural employment is likely to be small, however, because of the large size of the U.S. farm economy relative to U.S. agricultural trade with Canada and Mexico, the high capital intensity of U.S. agriculture, technological changes that have allowed production and trade to expand without requiring a substantial quantity of additional labor, and the offsetting effects on employment levels in different agricultural sectors.

The number of U.S. jobs supported by U.S. agricultural exports to Canada and Mexico has increased during the NAFTA period, in large part because these exports grew faster than labor productivity. Results from input-output analysis conducted by Persaud (2014) indicate that the total number of jobs (agricultural and nonagricultural) throughout the U.S. economy supported by each $1 billion in U.S. agricultural exports dropped from about 17,300 in 1994 to 6,577 in 2012. When one multiplies these numbers by the total value of U.S. agricultural exports to Canada and Mexico combined ($10.1 billion in 1994 and $39.5 billion in 2012), one finds that the number of jobs supported by these exports grew from about 175,000 to 260,000, an increase of 48 percent. By comparison, 142.5 million workers were employed in the U.S. economy in 2012, including 1.9 million in crop or animal production and another 1.7 million in food manufacturing (U.S. Department of Labor, Bureau of Labor Statistics, 2014).[13] Findings from two studies conducted early in the NAFTA period (Crawford and Link, 1997; Schluter and Gale, 1996) suggested that the agreement was not having a major effect on total U.S. agricultural employment at that time. These findings, whose underlying analysis considered the effects of both exports and imports on employment, are broadly consistent with an evaluation of NAFTA's impact on the U.S. economy as a whole by Arnold (2003). He found that the agreement increased the size of U.S. gross domestic product (GDP) by several hundredths of a percentage point.

With the liberalization of intraregional agricultural trade, the U.S. horticultural sector has seen both increased imports from the NAFTA countries and increased exports to those countries. The production data in table 3 and trade data in appendix tables 1-4 suggest that the experiences of U.S. horticultural producers in the face of this competition have varied by commodity. Of the 17 specific commodities whose production data for 1991-93 and 2010-12 are listed in table 3, increases in both production and area were recorded for six commodities: broccoli, onions, cranberries, sweet cherries, grapes, and strawberries. For all of these commodities except cranberries, U.S. exports to Canada averaged more than $75 million per year during 2011-13, and U.S. grape exports to Mexico also averaged more than $75 million during this period. Improved yields have made it possible for U.S.

production of some import-competing crops, such as bell peppers and watermelons, to increase during the NAFTA period, even though area harvested has declined. Still, U.S. producers of some horticultural crops, such as asparagus, cucumbers, and tomatoes, have found it challenging to compete with imports from the NAFTA countries, and both production and area harvested have declined.[14]

Table 3. U.S. production of vegetables, melons, and fruit has undergone many changes during the NAFTA era

Crop	Area harvested			Production			Yield		
	1991-93	2010-12	Change	1991-93	2010-12	Change	1991-93	2010-12	Change
	Hectares (thousands)		*Percent*	*Metric tons (thousands)*		*Percent*	*Metric tons per hectare*		*Percent*
Vegetables and melons, 24 crops	735.7	682.4	-7.3	15,212	19,834	30.4	206.8	290.7	40.6
Asparagus (1)	35.3	10.9	-69.2	103	36	-64.7	29.2	33.4	14.4
Bell peppers (1)	26.0	21.7	-16.6	635	797	25.5	243.8	366.8	50.5
Broccoli (1)	43.1	51.2	18.8	521	876	68.2	120.8	170.9	41.5
Cauliflower (1)	22.8	15.0	-34.3	313	309	-1.4	137.4	206.3	50.2
Chile peppers (1)	n.a.	8.8	n.a.	n.a.	200	n.a.	n.a.	226.6	n.a.
Cucumbers	22.9	17.7	-22.7	448	390	-13.0	195.8	220.4	12.6
Onions (1)	57.6	60.0	4.3	2,752	3,326	20.8	478.2	553.8	15.8
Tomatoes	53.3	39.4	-26.1	1,623	1,267	-21.9	304.4	321.7	5.7
Watermelons	83.4	51.7	-38.0	1,657	1,784	7.7	198.7	345.1	73.7
Crop	**Bearing area**			**Utilized production**			**Yield**		
Noncitrus fruit	808.8	812.0	0.4	14,944	16,170	8.2	18.5	19.9	7.8
Apples	183.5	134.9	-26.4	4,648	4,162	-10.5	25.3	30.8	21.7
Cranberries	11.7	15.8	35.0	187	341	82.9	15.9	21.6	35.5
Cherries, sweet	18.4	34.8	88.8	149	319	114.4	8.1	9.2	13.6
Cherries, tart	19.6	14.6	-25.6	115	75	-34.3	5.9	5.2	-11.8
Grapes	302.4	387.7	28.2	5,323	6,727	26.4	17.6	17.4	-1.4
Papayas (2), (3)	0.9	0.5	-43.2	29	13	-53.7	30.5	24.9	-18.6

Crop	Area harvested			Production			Yield		
	1991-93	2010-12	Change	1991-93	2010-12	Change	1991-93	2010-12	Change
	Hectares (thousands)		*Percent*	*Metric tons (thousands)*		*Percent*	*Metric tons per hectare*		*Percent*
Peaches	72.2	46.3	-35.9	1,130	949	-16.0	15.7	20.5	31.1
Pears	28.3	15.5	-45.4	839	797	-5.0	29.6	51.5	73.9
Strawberries (3)	19.9	23.0	15.4	621	1,326	113.5	31.1	57.7	85.1
Other noncitrus fruit	151.8	139.0	-8.5	1,903	1,458	-23.4	12.5	10.5	-16.3
Citrus fruit (4)	359.1	325.5	-9.4	11,765	10,479	-10.9	n.a.	n.a.	n.a.
Oranges (4), (5)	261.5	251.0	-4.0	8,412	7,934	-5.7	819.6	797.3	-2.7
Other citrus fruit (4)	97.6	74.4	-23.7	3,352	2,545	-24.1	n.a.	n.a.	n.a.

n.a. = not available.

NAFTA = North American Free Trade Agreement.

Note: Data are not collected for all States that might produce these crops. (1) Includes processing total for dual usage crops.

(2) Data listed for 2010-12 are actually for 2010-11 and cover Hawaii only.

(3) Data for area are for area harvested, not bearing area. Yields are based on utilized production.

(4) Data for citrus fruit correspond to crop years 1990-91 to 1992-93 and 2010-11 to 2012-13 and do not include limes. (5) Yield expressed in boxes per hectare. A box of oranges from Arizona or California weighs 75 pounds, 85 pounds from Texas, and 90 pounds from Florida.

Source: USDA, Economic Research Service, using USDA/NASS (2013a, 2013b, 2013c, 1994a, 1994b, 1993).

Processed Food Sector Features Substantial Levels of Foreign Investment

One of NAFTA's main objectives was to "increase substantially investment opportunities in the territories of the Parties" (see Article 102 of the agreement)—an objective that encompasses the promotion of FDI. As mentioned earlier, NAFTA instituted a number of key principles concerning the treatment of foreign investors in an effort to draw more FDI to the region.

For Mexico, these commitments reinforced similar changes made to its national laws and regulations as part of a long- term effort started in the 1980s to make the Mexican economy more attractive to foreign investors. With these investment rules firmly in place, Mexico's agricultural, food, beverage, and tobacco sectors attracted net inflows of additional FDI (from all countries) totaling $48.1 billion from 1999 to 2013, according to Mexican statistics (figure 3). Forty-nine percent ($23.6 billion) of these invest- ments were destined for the food industry, while only 2 percent ($976 million) were destined for production agriculture (crop and livestock production and agricultural services). The relatively small amount of FDI in production agriculture suggests that other methods, such as contracting, are used to structure cross-border business relationships between Mexican growers and U.S. buyers.

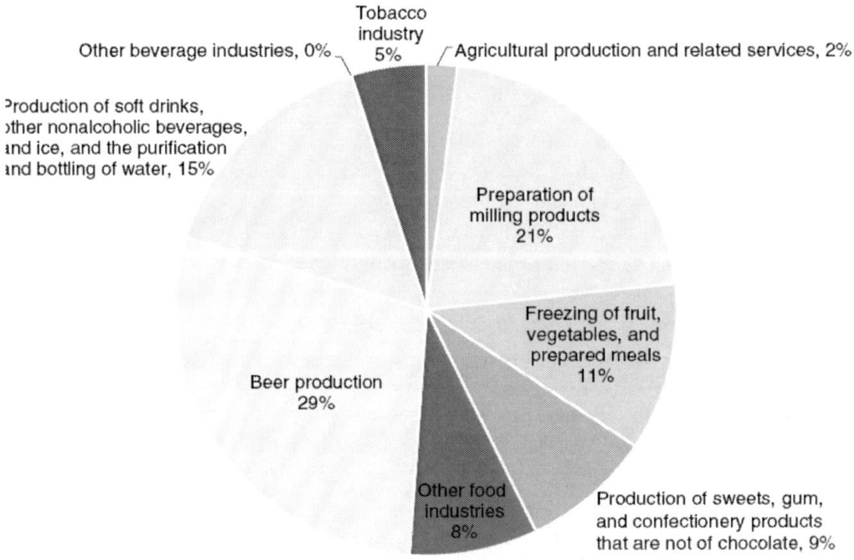

Notes: FDI= Foreign direct investment. Chart is based on the sectoral distribution of total net inflows ($48.1 billion) during 1999-2013.

Source: USDA, Economic Research Service, using data from México, Secretaría de Economía, Dirección General de Inversión Extranjera (2014).

Figure 3. Since 1999, the food industry has received about half of the net inflows of FDI in Mexico's agricultural, food, beverage, and tobacco sectors.

Changes in how the processed food sector is defined within U.S. FDI statistics, along with restrictions on disclosing data that could be used to identify individual firms, make it difficult to evaluate changes in FDI in the North American processed food sector since NAFTA's implementation. U.S. firms account for most of the FDI in the North American processed food sector, which is currently defined in U.S. statistics not to include the beverage industry or production agriculture. In 2013, the U.S. direct investment position (i.e., the total value of assets, on a historical-cost basis) in the processed food industries of Canada and Mexico equaled $10.1 billion and $4.0 billion, respectively.[15] In contrast, the Canadian and Mexican direct investment positions in the U.S. processed food industry were $1.8 billion and $2.1 billion, respectively. Food sales associated with U.S. direct investment in Canada and Mexico are substantial. In 2012, majority-owned affiliates of U.S. multinational food companies had sales of $32.4 billion in Canada and $13.8 billion in Mexico (figure 4). Together, these sales were 90 percent larger than the value of U.S. processed food exports to Canada and Mexico.

Prices Indicate That North American Markets Are Still Not Fully Integrated

Another sign of market integration is that a good sells for the same price at any location within that market at a given point in time—an economic concept called the "Law of One Price." With the elimination of the tariff and quotas that formerly governed intraregional trade, price differences across NAFTA countries are expected to be smaller, and national prices are expected to follow similar patterns in response to changing market conditions. Figure 5 provides a simple illustration of price integration in the U.S. and Mexican wheat markets. During the 3 years prior to NAFTA (1991-93), the Mexican price of wheat was over $100 per metric ton higher than the U.S. price. With the phasing out of the tariffs that formerly governed U.S.-Mexico wheat trade, this price difference gradually narrowed during NAFTA's first 8 years (1994-2001). Since then, U.S. and Mexican wheat prices have tended to move in tandem.

Empirical studies of price integration in the U.S. and Mexican markets suggest that one should not overgeneralize the presence of market integration in North American agriculture. In a study of U.S. and Mexican horticultural markets during the period January 1998 to September 2008, Avendaño Ruiz et al. (2014) find that binational integration is partial and varies from one commodity to another. Of the six commodities studied (avocados, cucumbers, onions, peppers, strawberries, and tomatoes), the U.S.-Mexican tomato market is shown to be the most integrated, followed by the markets for onions and peppers. In a study of U.S. and Mexican white corn prices during the period 1998-2005, Motamed et al. (2008) discover that U.S. and Mexican prices lack a common relationship over the long run.

Integration of agricultural markets within individual NAFTA countries may also be incomplete, particularly in Mexico where the level of economic development can vary substantially from one region to another. Of the six commodities studied by Avendaño Ruiz et al., the avocado market is the most integrated within Mexico, while the strawberry market is the most integrated within the United States. In the white corn study by Motamed et al., the researchers determine that state-level prices in Mexico do not respond strongly to a national price. Instead, they find that the prices of some states—the neighboring states of Chiapas and Oaxaca in the south, for instance—are closely related, while the prices of the two largest white corn-producing states—Sinaloa and Jalisco—affect prices in many other states.

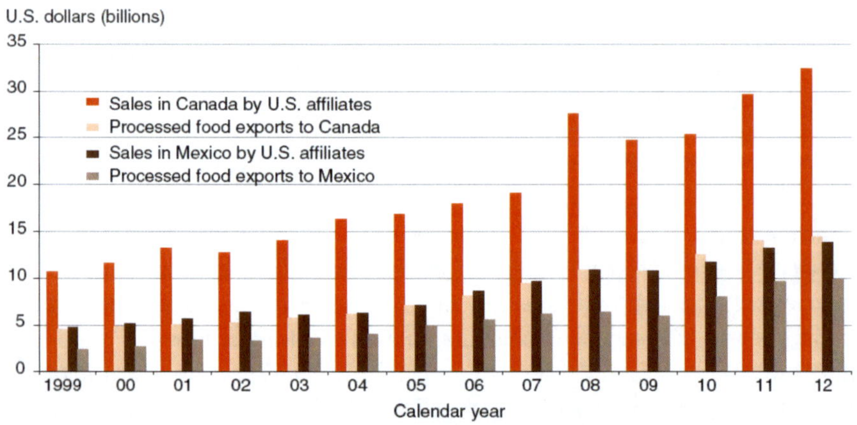

Note: Affiliate sales are those of nonbank majority-owned U.S. affiliates and do not include sales in the beverage industry.

Source: USDA, Economic Research Service, using data from U.S. Department of Commerce, Bureau of Economic Analysis (2014a) (affiliate sales) and USDA/FAS (2014a) (processed food exports).

Figure 4. Food sales by U.S.-owned affiliates in Canada and Mexico greatly exceed U.S. processed food exports to those countries.

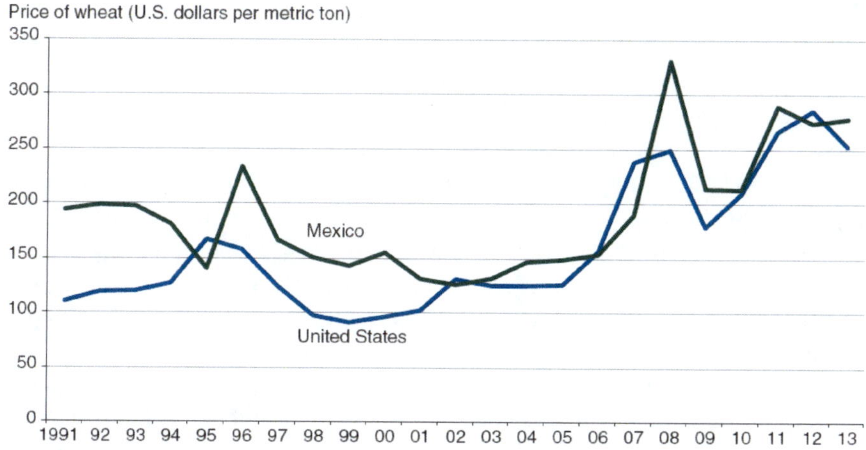

Notes: NAFTA = North American Free Trade Agreement. Years in figure correspond to agricultural years in Mexico and marketing years in the United States.
Source: USDA, Economic Research Service, using data from SAGARPA/SIAP (2014a); and USDA/NASS (2014b).

Figure 5. U.S. and Mexican wheat prices follow more similar patterns under NAFTA.

A North American Market for Grains, Oilseeds, and Related Products

Creation of a far more integrated North American market in grains, oilseeds, and related products is one of NAFTA's major achievements. For Mexico, NAFTA marked a transformation from the strict administration of imports via licensing requirements and the provision of guaranteed prices to domestic producers of many field crops to a system featuring duty-free trade with the United States and Canada and a mix of domestic agricultural supports similar to those in the United States. For the United States and Canada, trade liberalization of grains and oilseeds under NAFTA primarily involved the removal of minor tariffs on bilateral trade. Recent elimination of the single-desk trading status of the Canadian Wheat Board further advances the integration of the North American market.

Rising Demand for Feed and Food Drives Integration

Rising demand for feed and food has created new opportunities for intraregional trade in grains and oilseeds. Poultry and hog producers in Mexico, for instance, rely heavily on imported feedstuffs as they seek to meet their country's growing demand for meat. These imports come primarily from the United States, although Canada is a regular supplier to Mexico of rapeseed and rapeseed oil. In 2013, Mexico imported from Canada about 1.4 million metric tons of rapeseed and 23,000 metric tons of rapeseed oil. Because of growing feed demand in Mexico and the liberalization of U.S.- Mexico agricultural trade, U.S. exports to Mexico of feed grains, oilseeds, and related products increased from an annual average of 8.3 million metric tons during 1989-92 to 18.5 million metric tons per year during 2008-12 (figure 6).[16] In 2013, these exports dropped to 14.5 million metric tons due to the adverse effects of the 2012 drought on U.S. grain and oilseed production. To make up for this shortfall, Mexico increased its imports of corn and soybeans from South America.

Note: Feedstuffs are defined as encompassing the commodity groupings of feed grains and products, feeds and fodders (excluding oilcake), and oilseeds and products.

Source: USDA, Economic Research Service, using data from USDA/FAS (2014a) (exports) and SAGARPA/SIAP (2014b) (production).

Figure 6. U.S. feedstuffs are crucial to Mexican pork and poultry production.

Duty-free access to U.S. and Canadian feedstuffs enables Mexican livestock producers to expand output and lower their costs of production—thereby making possible a substantial increase in Mexican meat consumption. Between 1993 and 2013, per capita consumption in Mexico rose from 16 to 32 kilograms (an increase of 90 percent) for poultry meat (broiler plus turkey) and from 10 to 16 kilograms (60 percent) for pork.[17] Canada's poultry and hog producers also use some U.S. feedstuffs— most notably corn and soybean meal—and use of corn by Canada's ethanol producers has expanded, although growth of corn-based ethanol production in Canada is expected to slow (Ting, 2014).

A close examination of U.S. trade statistics (see app. tables 1-4) reveals that feedstuff trade among the NAFTA countries encompasses a diversity of products, in addition to traditional bulk commodities such as corn, sorghum, wheat, soybeans, rapeseed, and oilseed oils and meals. There is substantial two-way trade between Canada and the United States in mixed feeds and mixed feed ingredients other than pet food, as well as of U.S. exports to Mexico of preparations used for animal feeding (other than pet food and bird seed) and brewers' and distillers' dregs and waste. This latter category includes DDGS.

The quadrupling of U.S. wheat and rice exports to Mexico during the NAFTA period has helped to limit a decrease in Mexican wheat consumption and boost Mexican rice consumption. Mexico's population grew from 90 million to 119 million (33 percent) between 1993 and 2013, but the area planted with rice and wheat in Mexico is lower than it was during the early 1990s.[18] In 2013, annual per capita wheat consumption in Mexico equaled about 55 kilograms, 8 percent lower than in 1993, while per capita rice consumption equaled about 7.2 kilograms, 33 percent higher than in 1993. In 2013, U.S. rice exports to Mexico reached about 861,000 metric tons (product-weight basis), compared with 256,000 in 1993. Per capita rice consumption in Mexico is still low relative to other parts of Latin America, suggesting the possibility of further growth in U.S. rice exports to Mexico (Juarez, 2014).

U.S. Corn Exports to Mexico More Than Quadruple in Volume

NAFTA provided much of the legal framework for the expansion in U.S. corn exports to Mexico over the past two decades. Compared with their average annual volume during the decade prior to NAFTA (1984-93), these exports have more than quadrupled. The export volume for 2012, 10.1 million metric tons, included 8.5 million metric tons of conventional corn, 1.5 million metric tons of DDGS, and 129,000 metric tons of cracked corn, which consists of broken or ground kernels and is used to feed livestock (figure 7).[19] U.S. corn exports (including cracked corn and DDGS) to Mexico accounted for 31 percent of Mexico's supply during 2008-12, compared with 16 percent during 1984-93.[20] Yellow corn, used primarily to feed livestock or to manufacture starch, makes up the bulk of U.S. corn exports to Mexico. White corn, used mainly to make tortillas and other corn-based foods, accounted for about 7 percent of these exports during 2008-12.

Prior to NAFTA, Mexico strictly regulated corn imports through the use of licensing requirements. As part of NAFTA, Mexico established a set of transitional duty-free TRQs for U.S. and Canadian corn that gradually expanded during the period 1994-2007 and were finally eliminated in 2008. These TRQs were far too small to accommodate Mexico's growing demand for corn. To remedy this constraint, the Mexican Government customarily issued import permits beyond the amount required by NAFTA at tariff rates far below the over-quota tariff allowed by NAFTA, particularly for yellow corn.

Cracked corn was not covered by the transitional TRQs, and as recently as 2007, U.S. cracked corn exports to Mexico were as high as 2.7 million metric tons. With the end of NAFTA's transitional restrictions, Mexico's cracked corn imports have been replaced almost in their entirety by imports of conventional corn.

Mexican corn production has increased during the NAFTA period in response to rising feed demand for meat production and sustained levels of total corn demand for direct human consumption, although production tapered off during 2008-12 due to adverse weather conditions. Still, during that period, production was 58 percent higher than during 1984-93 (figure 8). Much of this increase stems from the devotion of more irrigated land to corn and the cultivation on those lands of new hybrids that provide yields comparable to those in the United States.

Rainfed cultivation of corn also has trended upward during the NAFTA period, due in part to yield improvements. Rainfed lands account for about 45 percent of Mexican corn production, and a year with unusually dry weather can negatively affect the country's total corn production, as was the case in Mexico's 2009 and 2011 agricultural years.

Barriers Removed From U.S.-Canada Trade in Wheat and Wheat Products

NAFTA contributed to expanded U.S.-Canada trade in wheat and wheat products (see app. Tables 1-2) by removing a number of significant barriers to this trade. The agreements eliminated the tariffs that formerly governed bilateral trade in wheat and wheat products, as well as Canada's licensing requirements for the importation of U.S. wheat and wheat products. Some of the tariffs in effect prior to 1989 discouraged bilateral trade. For instance, certain types of pasta traded between the two countries faced tariffs as high as 17.5 percent.

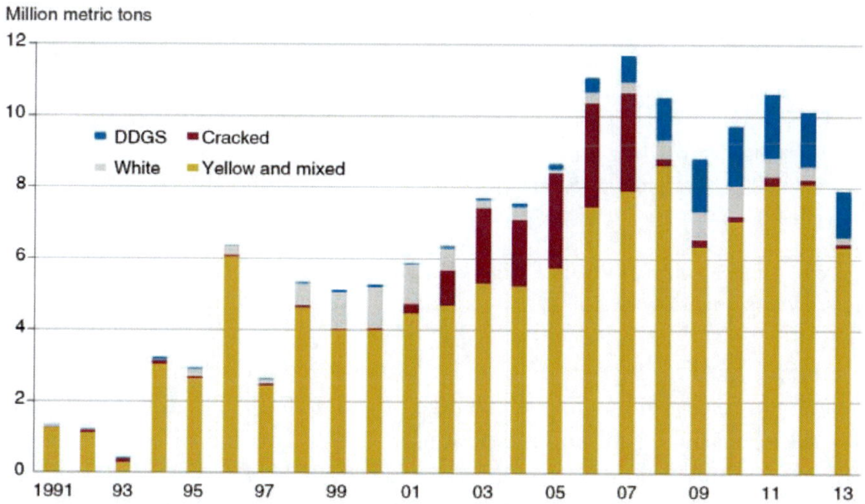

Notes: DDGS = distillers dried grains with solubles. Yellow and mixed corn exports are calculated by subtracting white corn exports from total corn exports. The harmonized tariff system defines DDGS and cracked corn (broken or ground kernels) as distinct commodities from corn.

Source: USDA, Economic Research Service, using data from U.S. Department of Commerce, Bureau of the Census, *Foreign Trade Statistics*, as cited by USDA/FAS (2014a) (total corn and cracked corn exports), and USDA/AMS (1991-2005, 2006-14) (white corn exports).

Figure 7. Distillers dried grains with solubles complement U.S. corn exports to Mexico.

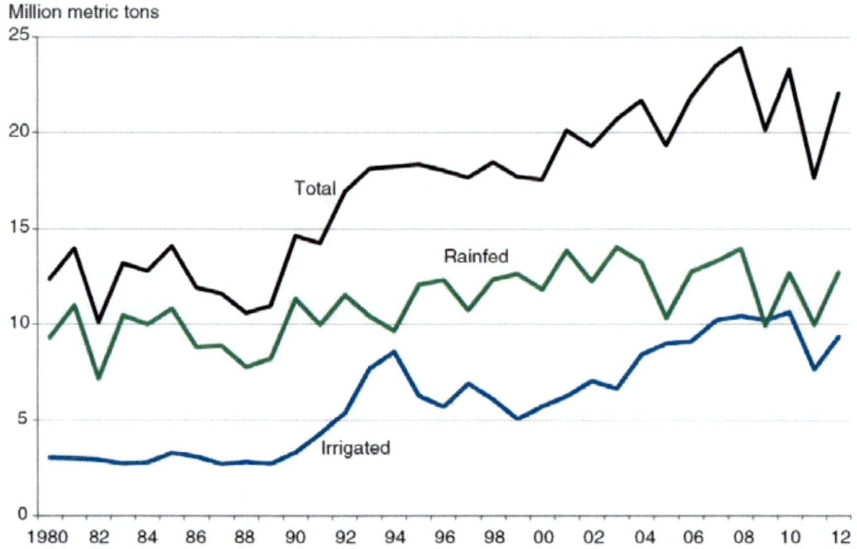

NAFTA = North American Free Trade Agreement.

Source: USDA, Economic Research Service, using data from SAGARPA/SIAP (2014a).

Figure 8. Mexican corn production has increased during the NAFTA period, although this growth is now slowing.

During the first 5 years of CUSTA (1989-93), U.S. wheat imports from Canada increased from an annual average of about 274,000 metric tons during 1984-88 to nearly 1.8 million metric tons in 1993. This increase was due not only to the trade policy changes fostered by CUSTA but also to new international trading rules within the URAA that required Canada to eliminate the transporta- tion subsidies provided under the Western Grain Transportation Act (WGTA) for moving grains from producing areas to the country's export terminals. Removal of these subsidies encouraged less of an east-west orientation and more of a north-south orientation for Canadian wheat shipments. A relatively weak Canadian dollar also played an important role in increased U.S. demand for Canadian wheat during the 1990s. Today, wheat from Canada is a small, routine component of the U.S. wheat supply. Canadian wheat exports to the United States averaged 2.4 million metric tons per year during 2009-13, accounting for about 3 percent of the U.S. supply.

Canadian Government Ends Canadian Wheat Board's Single-Desk Trading Status

In August 2012, the CWB lost its "single-desk" trading authority to operate a national monop- sony (i.e., single buyer) for wheat and barley produced in Alberta, Manitoba, Saskatchewan, and the Peace River District of British Columbia and destined for export or for human consumption in Canada, as the result of legislation enacted by the Canadian Government in December 2011. This legislation further requires that the CWB be privatized not later than 2016, and Canada's wheat and barley farmers have the option to decide whether to use the services of the CWB.

Although the end of the CWB's single-desk status and its transformation to a private-sector firm are not required by NAFTA, these developments increase the integration of North America's wheat and barley markets to a high level by enabling Canadian farmers to market their output through the private sector, much like their U.S. and Mexican counterparts. In addition, these reforms greatly change an institution that had been viewed by some participants in the sector as the source of unwelcome distortions in the international wheat market. For many years, the U.S. Government and the U.S. wheat industry argued that the CWB "took sales" from U.S. wheat producers through various noncommercial activities, including the cross-subsidization of sales among various buyers, the sale of wheat with higher protein content at the price of lower protein product, and the use of its special privileges, such as government support of its borrowing of funds, to generate a "financial cushion" to discount export prices (Goodloe, 2004; Schnepf, 2004).

The economic impacts of the CWB's reformation are still being evaluated. According to Carter and Loyns (1996), the end of the single desk would lead to higher farm prices for wheat and barley in Canada. Following record Canadian production of grain and oilseeds in 2013, wheat shipments via truck increased to points near the Manitoba/North Dakota border, a possible sign of a further strengthening of the north-south orientation to Canadian wheat trade or of rail congestion for west-bound shipments. Since the end of single-desk authority, Canadian grain farmers have focused more on developments other than the CWB's privatization, including the stresses placed on the country's grain handling and transportation system by record crops in 2013 and logistical problems resulting from adverse weather conditions (Ting, 2014).

NAFTA Facilitates Expansion of Canada's Rapeseed Sector

Trade liberalization under NAFTA has helped to facilitate a major development in Canadian agriculture—the emergence of a stronger and more vibrant rapeseed sector with a sizable presence in the North American oils market. Prior to 1989, the United States and Canada each maintained import tariffs on vegetable oils produced using the oilseed most commonly grown in the other country. Specifically, the United States applied rates of 7.5 percent on Canadian rapeseed oil, and Canada applied rates of 7.5 to 15.0 percent on U.S. soybean oil. These rates were high enough to discourage bilateral oil trade without prohibiting it altogether.

NAFTA's elimination of these import tariffs was timely for Canadian rapeseed growers, as a GM variety of rapeseed was approved by Canadian authorities in 1995. With duty-free access to the U.S. and Mexican vegetable oil markets, access to rapeseed varieties that were suited to the Canadian climate and easier to cultivate, elimination of the Gross Revenue Insurance Program (GRIP) that had held crop land in wheat production, and favorable prices for rapeseed compared with other crops, Canadian farmers devoted more land to rapeseed production. Between marketing years 1988/89 and 2014/15 (August to July), Canada's area harvested with rapeseed increased from 3.7 million hectares to 7.8 million hectares, while area harvested with wheat dropped from 12.9 million hectares to 9.3 million hectares (USDA/FAS, 2014b). The resulting increase in rapeseed production provided the basis for a large increase in Canadian rapeseed oil exports. In 2013, U.S. and Mexican imports of Canadian rapeseed oil equaled 1.3 million metric tons and 29,000 metric tons, respectively, with a combined value of $1.6 billion. By contrast, U.S. imports of rapeseed oil equaled 99,000 metric tons, with a value of $45 million, in 1988.

Livestock and Animal Product Markets Experience Further Integration

NAFTA has played an important role in advancing the formation of a single North American market for livestock and animal products, primarily by phasing out tariff and quota barriers governing intra-regional trade and by encouraging greater cooperation among the member governments on sanitary regulations. Among the more significant trade barriers eliminated by the two agreements were Mexico's import permit requirements for U.S. poultry meat and dairy products; Mexico's import tariffs on various livestock and animal products from Canada and the United States, which had rates as high as 20 percent; and the import quotas that formerly restricted U.S.-Canada trade in beef and in slaughter and feeder cattle.[21]

With the implementation of NAFTA, there are many signs of increased integration in North America's livestock and animal product markets. Between 1993 and 2013, annual intraregional trade in such products increased from $4.6 billion to $15.5 billion. Two-way trade in beef and pork between Canada and the United States and in beef between Mexico and the United States is an important component of this trade and occurs in much larger quantities than prior to NAFTA (app. tables 1-4). U.S. poultry meat and pork exports to Mexico are also substantial, averaging $1.0 billion and $891 million per year, respectively, during 2011-13. In addition, U.S. livestock producers purchase large numbers of hogs and cattle from Canada and cattle from Mexico for finishing and slaughter in the United States, with the resulting meat being sold either in the United States or abroad. However, Mexican and U.S. authorities have not yet negotiated a zoosanitary protocol that would allow Mexico to import slaughter cattle from the United States; numerous feed- lots in Mexico have expressed interest in such imports (Hernandez, et al., 2014).

NAFTA, however, did not liberalize trade in dairy, poultry, and egg products between Canada and the United States or between Canada and Mexico. For these products, Canada has a long-standing commitment to supply management—a production and management system that relies upon TRQs with prohibitively high over-quota tariffs as a means of strictly controlling import quantities. A future trade agreement involving the NAFTA countries—at either the multilateral, superregional, regional, or bilateral level—could conceivably broaden U.S. and Mexican access to Canada's dairy, poultry, and egg product markets. No such agreement has been secured, although these markets may be subject to discussions as part of the negotiations for the Trans-Pacific Partnership (TPP), which involves all three NAFTA countries plus nine other countries in the Pacific Rim. For those livestock and animal product sectors where intraregional free trade already exists, the key to further integration lies mainly in greater coordination of sanitary regulations, strengthening of effective control measures for prevention or elimination of animal diseases, including enhanced monitoring and surveillance, and the prevention of unjustified conditions that could lead to trade restrictions.

U.S. Nonfat Dry Milk and Chicken Leg Quarters Gain Duty-Free Access to Mexico

Two U.S. animal products—nonfat dry milk (NFDM) and chicken leg quarters (CLQs)—did not gain duty-free access to the Mexican market until January 1, 2008. NFDM is the leading U.S. dairy product exported to Mexico, and it is the only item among livestock and animal products that was subject to a 14-year (1994-2007) transitional TRQ under NAFTA. Trade liberalization has allowed U.S. dairy producers to respond to rising Mexican demand for NFDM, a product that tends not to be produced in large quantities in Mexico, except during the rainy season when fluid milk production is often higher (Hernandez et al., 2013: 7). During 2009-13, U.S. NFDM exports to Mexico averaged about 161,000 metric tons per year, compared with an annual average of about 40,000 metric tons during 1989-93 (the 5 years before NAFTA). There is no obvious seasonal pattern in this trade, suggesting that U.S. product broadly augments Mexico's NFDM supply, rather than complementing the domestic milk supply during those times of the year when production is customarily low.

The main buyers of NFDM in Mexico are private-sector processors who reconstitute the product and then sell it in the form of pasteurized or ultra-high-temperature (UHT) milk. Prior to 2006, LICONSA, a Mexican parastatal enterprise that provides nutritional assistance to low-income households, was the country's largest holder of NFDM stocks. Since then, LICONSA has shifted toward the purchase and distribution of fluid milk as a means of supporting domestic dairy production (Hernandez and Branson, 2011: 5, 9).

Although NAFTA's transition to free trade for U.S. poultry meat exports to Mexico ended on January 1, 2003, U.S. CLQ exports to Mexico were subject to a temporary safeguard TRQ that lasted until the start of 2008. This safeguard, intended to limit the quantity of CLQ sales beyond Mexico's border regions, was the product of a bilateral agreement signed by the U.S. and Mexican Governments in July 2003 at the encouragement of industry representatives and was not one of NAFTA's transitional restrictions. The end of the safeguard has allowed larger volumes of U.S. CLQs into the interior of Mexico. During 2009-13, Mexican imports of chicken legs, thighs, or legs and thighs in one piece (the category in the import data that includes CLQs) from the United States averaged 249,000 metric tons per year, compared with 173,000 metric tons in 2007, the last year of the safeguard. CLQs are an attractive and affordable product for consumers who wish to prepare a meal featuring chicken but not to purchase a whole chicken.

Rising Mexican imports of U.S. CLQs have been accompanied by allegations that some of these imports were priced below the U.S. cost of production. In February 2011, the Mexican Government launched a formal antidumping investigation of this subject, and in August 2012, it published its final decision: chicken leg and muscle imports from four suppliers who had cooperated with the investigation would be subject to an AD duty of 25.7 percent, while imports from other suppliers would be subject to a duty of 127.5 percent (México, Secretaría de Economía, 2012). However, the Mexican Government has opted not to apply these duties while Mexico's domestic poultry market stabilizes following outbreaks of HPAI in 2012 and 2013 (Hernandez and Branson, 2013). As of November 2014, Mexican authorities recognized 11 of Mexico's States as being free of both the H5N2 and H7N3 types of avian influenza (AI) (México, SAGARPA/SENASICA, Dirección General de Salud Animal, Dirección de Epidemiologia y Análisis de Riesgo, 2014).

Regionalization of Sanitary Standards Facilitates Meat Trade

Both Article 716 of NAFTA and Article 6 of the WTO Agreement on the Application of Sanitary and Phytosanitary Measures require, when possible, the regionalization of trade-related sanitary and phytosanitary standards. In the case of livestock and animal product trade, regionalization of sanitary standards allows exports to flow from regions within a country that are free of contagious foreign animal diseases, even if those diseases are endemic in another part of that country. Once an outbreak of a specific animal disease is identified, the national government of the importing country makes a risk assessment to determine if trade restrictions can be defined along regional lines in such a way that international trade may continue. Recognition of a disease-free or low-risk region, however, does not guarantee that meat processors in that region will be allowed to export their product. Processors also must be certified by their national governments as being eligible to export and may be subject to audits by the importing country's government.[22] Such audits sometimes result in the decertification of individual meat processing plants, either on a temporary or a permanent basis.

Regionalization is an important facilitator of meat trade. With respect to U.S.-Canada trade, the definition of Canada as a minimal-risk region for bovine spongiform encephalopathy (BSE) by U.S. regulators in 2004 led to the resumption of Canadian cattle and beef exports to the United States several years later. As part of activities organized under through the Canada-U.S. Regulatory Cooperation Council (RCC), the Canadian Food Inspection Agency (CFIA) and USDA's Animal and Plant Health Inspection Service (APHIS) have prioritized its efforts to recognize each other's zoning decisions if a foreign animal disease outbreak, such as foot-and-mouth disease (FMD) or another highly contagious foreign animal disease, were to occur in either country. The APHIS-CFIA team is establishing a framework mechanism to minimize trade disruptions while safeguarding animal health in both countries.

With respect to U.S.-Mexico trade, regionalization has enabled U.S. poultry meat exports to Mexico to continue largely uninterrupted in the face of localized outbreaks of low pathogenic AI in specific counties in the States of Minnesota, Kentucky, and Tennessee in 2009 (San Juan, 2009; Williams, 2009; San Juan, 2010) and Missouri in 2011 (Branson, 2011). In addition, Mexican authorities have worked with their U.S. counterparts to regionalize U.S. sanitary standards related to Classical Swine Fever (CSF) and Exotic Newcastle Disease (END). This effort has fostered modest levels of Mexican pork and poultry meat exports to the United States, but the opportunities to export fresh or frozen product to the United States are still limited, discussed in the next paragraph. In 2013, U.S. imports of pork and poultry meat from Mexico equaled about $22 million (6,000 metric tons) and $14 million (4,000 metric tons), respectively. Unprocessed frozen product other than carcasses, half carcasses, and hams, shoulders, and cuts thereof with bone in accounts for most of the pork imports from Mexico, while prepared meals of chicken account for most of the poultry meat imports. Mexico is a far more active exporter of pork to Japan and South Korea. Such exports totaled $411 million (76,000 metric tons) in 2013.

The U.S. and Mexican governments currently do not share the same assessment of the sanitary situation in Mexico with respect to CSF and END. As of September 2014, the United States recognizes nine Mexican States—Baja California, Baja California Sur, Campeche, Chihuahua, Nayarit, Quintana Roo, Sinaloa, Sonora, and Yucatán—as being free of CSF and lists those States as eligible to export raw pork to the United States under certain conditions (USDA/APHIS, 2014a; USDA/ FSIS, 2014). In addition, the United States recognizes three Mexican States—Campeche, Quintana Roo, and Yucatán—as being free of END and lists two specific meat-processing establishments in Mexico as being eligible to export raw poultry to the United States, but only if that poultry originated in the United States or another END-free country eligible to export to the United States (USDA/APHIS, 2014a;

USDA, FSIS, 2014). All regions in Mexico are eligible to export processed pork and poultry meat to the United States.

Mexican authorities state that they have much wider geographic control over CSF and END. In January 2009, the Mexican Government declared its entire territory to be free of CSF following a nationwide eradication campaign, and in July 2013, it recognized all of Mexico to be free of END (México, SAGARPA/SENASICA, Dirección General de Salud Animal, Dirección de Epidemiologia y Análisis de Riesgo, 2014). By comparison, the United States considers CSF to have been eradicated within the United States and Canada, with the last outbreak of END in the United States occurring during 2002-03. Industry sources cited by Hernandez (2003) believe that recognition of Mexico as being free or at low risk of CSF would lead to expanded access for Mexican pork not only in the U.S. market but also elsewhere, while recognition of Mexico as being disease free of END and AI would allow U.S. processors to use broilers originating and slaughtered in Mexico (Hernandez, et al., 2014).

In response to requests submitted by the Mexican Government in 2007, 2008, and 2009 seeking recognition of CSF-free status in an increasingly larger number of Mexican States and finally all of Mexico, USDA/APHIS (2014b) published a proposed rule that would define a new region in Mexico as being of low risk of CSF. This new region would consist of all Mexican States that APHIS does not recognize as CSF-free, except for the State of Chiapas. The proposed rule would allow the importation of fresh pork and pork products from the low-risk region under certain conditions. For instance, the pork would need to be obtained from swine raised on farms where CSF antigen exposure has not been detected and contained in such a fashion as to prevent exposure to other swine, wildlife, and swine products. In the proposed rule, APHIS explained its reasoning for not recognizing all of Mexico as CSF-free, based on an assessment of the risk of CSF spreading to the U.S. swine population via the importation of pork and pork products from the Mexican States not recognized by APHIS as CSF-free. Risk factors identified include "serologic evidence, found in some Mexican States as recently as 2012, of exposure to swine to the CSF virus"; "the lack of uniformity in the quality of epidemiological investigations of CSF suspect cases in Mexico"; and "the existence of common land borders between some Mexican States and neighboring CSF-affected countries" (USDA/APHIS, 2014b).

Trade Liberalization and Sanitary Cooperation Facilitate Beef Exports to Non-NAFTA Countries

Trade liberalization and sanitary cooperation among the NAFTA countries have strengthened the ability of North American beef producers to compete in markets outside the NAFTA region. Upon NAFTA's implementation in 1994, the member countries immediately removed all remaining tariff and quota barriers to intraregional trade in cattle and beef, a policy change that has allowed such trade to grow well beyond previous levels.[23] Moreover, NAFTA gives cattle producers in each member country duty-free access to the full range of feedstuffs, livestock, and other inputs produced in the North American free-trade area, enabling North American beef to be more competitive in quality and price. For Mexican producers, this development has facilitated the emergence of a larger feedlot sector, the compression of beef production timelines, the production of lean beef with a smoother texture, and an increase in beef exports (Peel et al., 2011). In 2013, Mexico exported about 129,000 metric tons ($701 million) of beef—primarily to the United States, in part due to drought-related declines in U.S. production. In 1993, U.S. beef imports from Mexico equaled 1,000 metric tons ($3 million).

The NAFTA countries have a long history of cooperating on sanitary issues involving livestock and animal products. Perhaps the most important example over the past two decades is the establishment of greater control over the risk factors associated with BSE.[24] In response to the discovery of this disease in Canada in May 2003 and in the United States in December 2003,[25] a number of countries within and outside of NAFTA imposed sanitary restrictions on cattle and beef from Canada and, to a lesser extent, the United States. In the years that followed the BSE discoveries, the NAFTA governments made a concerted effort to coordinate their sanitary policies related to BSE, to upgrade international standards in this area, and to modify their sanitary requirements gradually for specific types of cattle and beef, usually based on the age of the animal, in order to achieve the resumption of intraregional trade in cattle and beef.[26] The modification of Mexican regulations in April 2014 to allow the importation of beef and beef by-products obtained from U.S. cattle of any age is the most recent step toward the normalization of this trade (Branson and Hernandez, 2014).

Efforts toward the reestablishment of intraregional cattle and beef trade were accompanied by concomitant work to regain U.S. and Canadian access to the beef markets of non-NAFTA countries, such as Japan, Hong Kong, South Korea, and Taiwan, which had imposed import bans on U.S. and Canadian beef following the BSE detections. Both U.S. and Canadian beef exports to non-NAFTA countries have surpassed the levels that existed prior to the BSE findings, an indication that the industry has largely recovered from BSE-related disruptions. In 2013, U.S. beef exports to non- NAFTA countries equaled 565,000 metric tons, 5 percent higher than in 2002 (the year before the BSE discoveries); Canadian beef exports to non-NAFTA countries reached 43,000 metric tons, 39 percent higher than in 2002.

The immediate prospects for North American beef exports are constrained by supply factors, as cattle inventories in all three NAFTA countries have decreased. At the start of 2014, beef cattle inventories were 22 percent lower than their 2002 level in the United States, 16 percent lower in Canada, and 33 percent lower in Mexico (USDA/FAS, 2014b). High grain prices over the past several years have discouraged producers from increasing their herds. Industry consolidation in Canada has contributed further to lower herd numbers, while periods of drought in several cattle- producing regions in the United States and Mexico have deteriorated pasture conditions. While dry pastures in Mexico led to a short-term increase of feeder cattle exports to the United States in 2011 and 2012, Mexican herds declined significantly, lowering important supplies of feeder cattle for the Southwestern United States.

WTO Dispute on Country-of-Origin Labeling Moves to Compliance Proceedings

Concerns about the effects of mandatory country-of-origin labeling (COOL) by the United States on the integration of U.S. and Mexican cattle production, U.S. and Canadian cattle production, and U.S. and Canadian hog production are at the center of the Canadian and Mexican disputes with U.S. COOL requirements at the World Trade Organization (WTO). Mandatory COOL provides U.S. consumers with greater information about the geographic origin of their retail food purchases. Specifically, U.S. retailers are required to provide COOL for the following products: muscle cuts of beef (including veal), lamb (including mutton), pork, chicken, and goat; ground meat (beef, lamb, pork, chicken, or goat); peanuts, pecans, ginseng, and macadamia nuts; perishable agricultural commodities (i.e., fresh or frozen fruit and vegetables); and wild and farm-raised fish and shellfish.

The United States imports live cattle from Mexico and Canada and live hogs from Canada for finishing or immediate slaughter. Mexico has exported feeder cattle to the United States on a regular basis for over a quarter century

(Mitchell et al., 2001). In 2013, Mexican cattle exports to the United States equaled about 989,000 head, most of which were feeder animals. This number fluctuates from year to year and has averaged 1.2 million head per year since 2000. Market conditions and weather, especially drought, significantly affect the number of feeder cattle imported by the United States from Mexico in any given year.

Canada exports large numbers of both live cattle and live hogs to the United States for growing, finishing, and slaughter. Following the steady decline in Canadian cattle inventories from 2005 to 2011 and in Canadian hog inventories from 2006 to 2009, these exports are now smaller than when the decline in inventories was in full swing. Between 2008 and 2013, Canadian cattle exports to the United States decreased from 1.2 million to 1.0 million head, while corresponding hog exports decreased from 9.3 million to 5.0 million.

Implementation of mandatory COOL is the responsibility of USDA's Agricultural Marketing Service (AMS). The final rule originally applicable to muscle cuts and ground meat took effect on March 16, 2009 (table 4) and was contested soon after by the Canadian and Mexican Governments, which filed separate complaints at the WTO alleging that the labeling requirements were inconsis- tent with U.S. obligations under international trade agreements. In November 2009, a single panel was established to examine the complaints. In November 2011, a panel report was circulated to members—finding, among other things, that the requirements violated Article 2.1 of the WTO's Technical Barriers to Trade (TBT) Agreement by giving less favorable treatment to imported cattle and hogs from Canada and imported cattle from Mexico relative to like domestic product. The panel also found that the requirements violated Article 2.2 of the TBT Agreement by not fulfilling their legitimate objective of providing consumers with origin information.

In March 2012, each NAFTA country notified the WTO's Dispute Settlement Body (DSB) of its intention to appeal some of the panel's findings. The Appellate Body's report was circulated on June 29, 2012. In that report, the Appellate Body upheld the finding that the law offered less favorable treatment to Canadian cattle and hog producers and Mexican cattle producers because of increased recordkeeping and verification requirements. However, the Appellate Body reversed the finding that mandatory COOL was inconsistent with Article 2.2, under the reasoning that "the COOL measure does contribute, at least to some extent, to achieving its objective." Instead, the Appellate Body alleged that the origin information provided to consumers was far less than the amount of information collected from producers.

Table 4. The United States issued a new final rule for mandatory country-of-origin labeling in response to a WTO ruling

Product	Final Rule that took effect March 16, 2009	Final Rule that took effect May 23, 2013
Muscle cuts from animals born, raised, and slaughtered in the United States	"Product of U.S.A."	"Born (Hatched), Raised, and Slaughtered in the U.S."
Muscle cuts from animals born, raised, and slaughtered outside the United States	"Product of Country X"	Same as in 2009 Final Rule
Muscle cuts from animals born and raised outside the United States and slaughtered in the United States	"Product of Country X and the U.S.A."	"Born and Raised in Country X, Slaughtered in the United States"
Muscle cuts from animals born outside the United States but raised and slaugh- tered in the United States	"Product of U.S.A., Country X, and Country Y (as applicable)," where Country X (or Y) designate the country of birth.	"Born in Country X, Raised and Slaughtered in the United States"
Muscle cuts from animals born and raised outside the United States and slaughtered in the United States, com- ingled in a single production day with muscle cuts from animals born, raised, and slaughtered in the United States	"Product of U.S.A., Country X, and Country Y (as applicable)"	Such comingling is no longer allowed under the 2013 rule
Ground meat	Retailer must identify all countries where product originated or all reasonably pos- sible countries where product may have originated	Same as in 2009 Final Rule

Sources: USDA, Economic Research Service, using USDA, Agricultural Marketing Service (2009, 2013).

As the United States informed the DSB of its intention to implement the Appellate Body's findings, AMS issued a new final rule for muscle cuts that took effect on May 23, 2013 (table 4). The new rule requires labeling of muscle cuts to indicate clearly the country in which each major step in production (born, raised, and slaughtered) occurred. In addition, the new rule prohibits the comingling of muscle cuts from animals of different national origins if slaughtered during the same production day at the same facility; such comingling was allowed under the 2009 final rule. Canada and Mexico, however, disagreed with the U.S. position that the new rule had brought the United States into full compliance with the DSB's recommendations and rulings. Citing further harm, Canada and Mexico requested that a compliance panel be assembled. A WTO resolution was provided to the three governments in July 2014, and the compliance panel's report was circulated to WTO Members in October 2014. According to a summary provided by the WTO, the report indicates that the detrimental effect of the Final Rule's "labelling and recordkeeping requirements could not be explained by the need to convey to consumers information regarding the countries where livestock were born, raised, and slaughtered" (World Trade Organization, 2014a). In November 2014, the United States filed an appeal of the ruling.

A Highly Integrated Fruit and Vegetable Market

Trade liberalization under NAFTA, along with cooperation on phytosanitary issues, has helped to raise the integration of North America's fruit and vegetable markets from a medium to a high level. Many aspects of intraregional fruit and vegetable trade have been free of tariffs and quotas for more than a decade, and with the removal of NAFTA's last set of agricultural trade restrictions in 2008, regional fruit and vegetable trade is now free of such obstructions.

Intraregional fruit and vegetable trade has increased substantially since the implementation of NAFTA, and Mexican growers in particular have benefited from this expansion (figure 9). Mexico's annual exports of fruit and vegetables to the United States (including juice)[27] have more than tripled during the NAFTA period, approaching $9.4 billion in 2013. These exports have their roots in the development and growth over the past half century of a vibrant Mexican fruit and vegetable sector that is strongly oriented toward the U.S. market. Many of the U.S. import tariffs on Mexican produce in effect prior to NAFTA were designed on a seasonal basis (i.e., they were scheduled for the part of the year when U.S. production was on the market). Some of these tariffs were quite high. For example, Mexican asparagus faced a seasonal tariff of 25 percent.

Annual U.S. fruit and vegetable exports to Mexico also have more than tripled under NAFTA, reaching about $1.4 billion in 2013. These exports have benefited from the rapid expansion of Mexico's supermarket sector during the NAFTA period. Several U.S. supermarket chains operate in Mexico. As of November 2014, Texas-based H-E-B had a total of 43 stores in the Mexican States of Coahuila, Guanajuato, Nuevo León, San Luis Potosí, and Tamaulipas (Supermercados Internacionales H-E-B, 2014), and Wal-Mart was operating 2,114 stores throughout Mexico with formats including grocery sales (Wal-Mart de México y Centroamérica, 2014). Mexican super- market chains also purchase large quantities of U.S. produce.

Completion of U.S.-Canada trade liberalization for fruit and vegetables, along with broader applica- tion of greenhouse technologies to Canadian vegetable production, has fostered greater integration of the two countries' fruit and vegetable markets. At the aggregate level, U.S. fruit and vegetable imports from Canada have grown substantially during the NAFTA period. In 2013, these imports equaled $3.1 billion, compared with $213 million in 1988 and $318 million in 1993. At the commodity level, Canada has emerged as an important supplier to the United States of fresh greenhouse tomatoes, peppers, and cucumbers; fresh-market mushrooms; and fresh and frozen potatoes (app. table 2). U.S. tariffs on Canadian fruit and vegetables were generally small prior to 1989, with the exception of fresh mushrooms, which faced restrictions with an ad valorem tariff equivalent of about 28 percent on a trade-weighted, annual basis. U.S. growers have been active in the Canadian market for some time, particularly during the winter months. In 2013, U.S. fruit and vegetable exports to Canada approached $5.8 billion, compared with $639 million in 1988 and $1.9 billion in 1993.

The establishment of phytosanitary protocols during the NAFTA period for the importation of fresh avocados from Mexico has enabled this product to become a major component of intraregional agricultural trade. In 2013, U.S. fresh avocado imports from Mexico totaled about 510,000 metric tons, with a value of $992 million, and Canadian fresh avocado imports from Mexico totaled 46,000 metric tons, with a value of $115 million. Currently, the United States only allows the importation of Mexican fresh avocados from 24 municipalities in the State of Michoacán, but avocado producers in other Mexican States have expressed interest in being certified to export to the

United States, an activity that would require the establishment of appropriate phytosanitary protocols (Flores and Olson, 2013a).

Establishment of trade-facilitating phytosanitary protocols is also important for U.S. produce growers. In May 2014, for example, Mexico's National Service of Agrifood Health, Safety, and Quality (SENASICA) published procedural requirements that allow U.S. table stock potatoes and potatoes for processing to exported to any part of Mexico. This issue had been the subject of negotiations by the U.S. and Mexican Governments over a 10-year period, as previous rules only allowed for such products to be imported into the 16-mile zone immediately along the U.S.-Mexico border (Olson and Flores, 2014). Several weeks after the new procedural requirements took effect, however, a Mexican District Court Judge in Los Mochis, Sinaloa, issued an injunction that indefinitely suspended their implementation—a ruling that was based on a perceived lack of scientific evidence regarding the safety of U.S. potatoes with respect to the possible introduction of pests to Mexican agriculture and the environment (Olson, 2014).

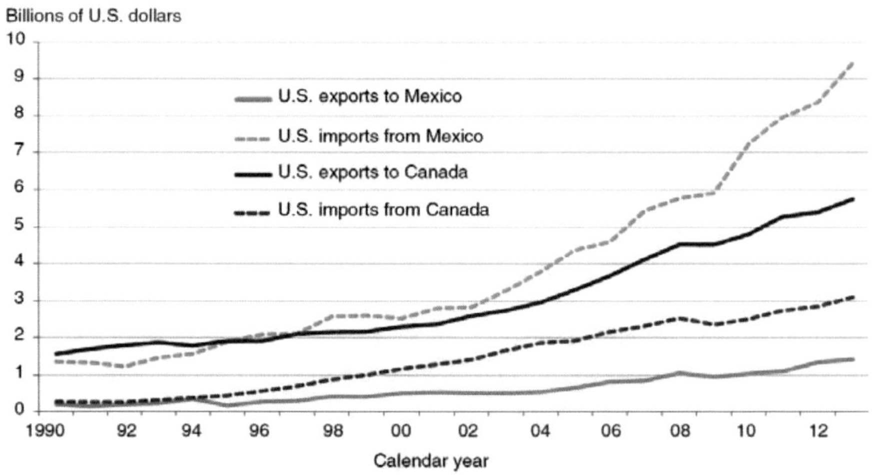

Notes: NAFTA = North American Free Trade Agreement.
Trade data in this figure include juice.
Source: USDA, Economic Research Service using data from USDA/FAS (2014a).

Figure 9. U.S. fruit and vegetable trade with Canada and Mexico has grown substantially during the NAFTA period.

Importance of Imports to U.S. Fruit and Vegetable Supply Increases

As a result of the heightened integration of North America's fruit and vegetable market, imports from the NAFTA countries have increased in their share of the U.S. fruit and vegetable supply. In 2011, Mexico and Canada combined supplied about 13 percent of the fresh or frozen fruit available in the United States and 17 percent of the available fresh or frozen vegetables. In 1990, these shares each equaled 6 percent. By comparison, countries outside NAFTA supplied 39 percent of the available fresh or frozen fruit in 2012 and 3 percent of the available fresh or frozen vegetables. In 1990, these shares equaled 29 percent and 1 percent, respectively. Changing diets and the development of off-season supplies of fresh produce outside the United States have fostered a shift in U.S. consumption away from processed fruits and vegetables and toward fresh produce. In 2011, fresh produce accounted for 50 percent of the U.S. fruit and vegetable supply (excluding juice), up from 45 percent in 1990.[28]

Net imports (i.e., imports minus exports) provide further evidence of the increased reliance on imports to meet U.S. fruit and vegetable demand (table 5). Prior to NAFTA, net imports from Mexico exceeded 15 percent of the U.S. supply for a wide variety of produce, including fresh tropical fruit with little U.S. production (limes, fresh mangos, and fresh papayas), fresh asparagus, broccoli and cauliflower for processing, chile peppers, fresh cucumbers, squash, and fresh tomatoes. Since NAFTA's implementation, several of these commodities—fresh limes, fresh papayas, watermelon, squash, and fresh tomatoes—increased by at least 10 percentage points in this measure. Net imports from Canada now account for a larger portion of the U.S. supply of bell peppers, fresh cucumbers, and fresh tomatoes than they did in the early 1990s due to the growth of the Canadian greenhouse industry. Net imports divided by U.S. disappearance are negative for those commodities where the United States is a net exporter to the trade partner in question (i.e., the world, Mexico, or Canada). For instance, during 2010-12, U.S. cantaloupe exports to Canada averaged about 229,000 metric tons per year, while corresponding imports averaged less than 1,000 metric tons per year. The resulting net exports (about 229,000 metric tons) corresponded to about 20 percent of U.S. disappearance of cantaloupe.

Table 5. Net imports from Mexico and Canada now account for a larger share of the availability of certain fruit and vegetables in the United States than they did before NAFTA

Commodity	Net imports divided by U.S. disappearance						Per capita use	
	from world		from Mexico		from Canada		Average	
	1991-93	2010-12	1991-93	2010-12	1991-93	2010-12	1991-93	2010-12
	Percent						*Kilograms*	
Selected fruit:								
Avocados, fresh[1]	4	64	0	49	-2	-6	0.7	2.0
Cantaloupe	19	29	11	-0	-4	-20	3.9	3.7
Grapes, fresh[1]	15	21	4	9	-13	-8	3.4	3.6
Limes, fresh[1]	66	100	82	98	-3	-0	0.4	1.2
Mangos, fresh[2]	92	100	85	67	-2	-0	0.4	1.1
Papayas, fresh	8	94	27	72	-9	-2	0.1	0.5
Strawberries, fresh	-8	-1	2	11	-9	-11	1.6	3.4
Watermelon	1	15	5	20	-5	-7	6.3	6.8
Selected vegetables:								
Asparagus, fresh	12	85	30	46	-13	-1	0.3	0.7
Bell peppers	24	48	11	49	-7	3	2.5	4.9
Broccoli and cauliflower, processing[3]	66	94	31	57	0	0	1.4	1.3
Chile peppers	35	79	16	42	-3	-0	2.3	3.1
Cucumbers, fresh	28	60	31	51	-6	6	2.2	3.2
Eggplant	19	43	34	44	-15	-8	0.2	0.4
Mushrooms, fresh[1]	-3	8	-0	1	-2	5	0.9	1.2
Onions, fresh	2	3	7	7	-4	-3	7.4	8.8
Potatoes, fresh	1	-0	-0	-2	1	3	22.5	16.1
Snap beans, fresh	-4	13	6	15	-10	-6	0.6	0.9
Squash[4]	23	50	19	42	-1	-1	1.7	2.0
Tomatoes, fresh	9	48	16	15	-7	2	7.1	9.3

[1] For these commodities, marketing years 1990/91, 1991/92, and 1992/93 are compared with marketing years 2009/10, 2010/11, and 2011/12.

[2] Net imports also include mangosteens and guavas and some dried product.

[3] Exports are assumed to equal zero in the net import calculations.
[4] Squash exports are estimated as 5 percent of miscellaneous vegetable exports in the net import calculations.
Sources: USDA, Economic Research Service presentation of data from Thornsbury, et al. (2014) (vegetable data); Perez and Plattner (2013) (fruit data); and USDA/FAS (2014a) (trade data).

U.S. Dry Beans Constitute a Larger and Steadier Portion of Mexican Supply

Dry beans are the main commodity among fruit and vegetables[29] for which transitional restrictions under NAFTA were eliminated on January 1, 2008. For the period 1994-2007, NAFTA specified gradually less restrictive TRQs for U.S. and Canadian exports to Mexico of dry beans belonging to the species *Phaseolus vulgaris*, or "common" beans. Common beans encompass many varieties, including black, pinto, kidney, navy, Great Northern, small white, pink, cranberry, and small red beans. Prior to NAFTA, Mexico tightly controlled the importation of dry beans through the use of import licensing.

Trade liberalization under NAFTA has enabled U.S. dry beans to account for a larger and steadier portion of Mexico's dry bean supply, although exports still continue to fluctuate due to weather-related conditions affecting production in either country (figure 10). During marketing years (MYs) 2009/10 to 2013/14 (September 2009 to August 2014), imports from the United States accounted for about 11 percent of Mexico's dry bean supply (when calculated as imports divided by the sum of domestic production and total imports from all countries), compared with 5 percent during MYs 1988/89 to 1992/93. U.S. exports of dry common beans to Mexico averaged equaled about 126,000 metric tons per year during MYs 2009/10 to 2013/14, compared with 62,000 metric tons during MYs 1988/89 to 1992/93.[30]

Implementation of FDA Food Safety Modernization Act Moves Forward

In January 2011, President Obama signed into law the FDA Food Safety Modernization Act (FSMA), which makes a number of significant regulatory changes concerning fruit and vegetable production and trade. In the United States, the U.S. Food and Drug Administration (FDA) is the Federal agency with primary responsibility for ensuring the safety of domestic and imported fresh produce.[31] Article 712 of NAFTA recognizes the right of each member country to use sanitary and phytosanitary measures "in order to protect human, animal, or plant life or health in its territory," as long as those measures are based on scientific principles, do not discriminate among the NAFTA partners, and are not trade restrictions in disguise.[32]

FSMA contains many provisions that are likely to affect fruit and vegetable trade with Canada and Mexico, four of which are discussed here. First, FSMA requires the FDA to adopt regulations providing for minimum science-based standards for the safe production and harvesting of those types of fruit and vegetables that are raw agricultural commodities for which the FDA determines that such standards would minimize the risk of serious adverse health consequences or death. To this end, the FDA issued a Proposed Rule for Produce Safety (Standards for the Growing, Harvesting, Packing, and Holding of Produce for Human Consumption) in January 2013. The Proposed Rule addresses various identified routes of microbial contamination of produce, including agricultural water, biological soil amendments of animal origin, health and hygiene of farm personnel, domesticated and wild animals, and equipment, tools, and buildings. It also contains provisions covering the topics of sprouts and personnel training (FDA, 2013a).

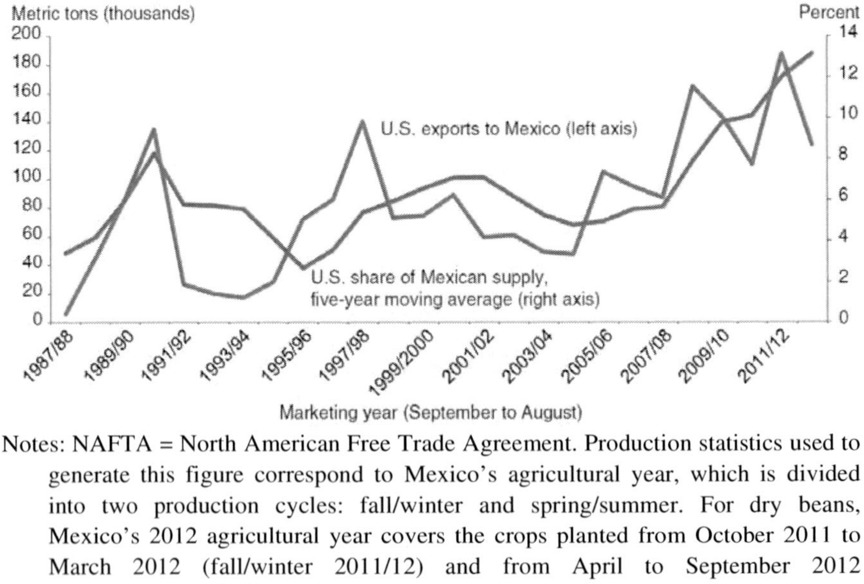

Notes: NAFTA = North American Free Trade Agreement. Production statistics used to generate this figure correspond to Mexico's agricultural year, which is divided into two production cycles: fall/winter and spring/summer. For dry beans, Mexico's 2012 agricultural year covers the crops planted from October 2011 to March 2012 (fall/winter 2011/12) and from April to September 2012 (spring/summer 2012).

To compare U.S. exports with Mexican production, we matched U.S. marketing years and Mexican agricultural years so that the starting year of the marketing year is the same number that denotes the agricultural year. For instance, U.S. marketing year 2012/13 is matched with Mexico's 2012 agricultural year. This enables us to compare the quantities of U.S. and Mexican dry beans that are on the market at roughly the same time.

Source: USDA, Economic Research Service, using data from USDA/FAS (2014a) and SAGARPA/SIAP (2014a).

Figure 10. NAFTA has enabled U.S. dry common beans to become a larger portion of Mexican supply.

The FDA extended the deadline for comments on the Proposed Rule for Produce Safety and received a great deal of feedback from the private sector and research community, particularly with respect to the Proposed Rule's possible effects on farms of different sizes. In response, the FDA decided to revise parts of the proposed rule—including the sections on water quality standards and testing, standards for using raw manure and compost, the definition of a farm, and procedures for withdrawing the qualified exemption for certain farms (Taylor, 2013). In September 2014, the FDA published its revised Proposed Rule for Produce Safety and solicited further comments on these revisions (FDA, 2014b).

To avoid placing an undue burden on smaller farms and food producers, the FDA proposed an outright exemption from the Produce Rule for those farms with average annual produce sales during the previous 3 years of $25,000 or less (on a rolling basis), while FSMA itself specifies a qualified exemption for other growers. To qualify for this exemption in a given calendar year, a farm must meet both of the following conditions: (1) the farm's total food sales during the previous 3 years were valued at an annual average less than $500,000, adjusted for inflation; and (2) more than half of the farm's total food sales during the previous 3 years were made directly to "qualified end users"—defined by FSMA to include (a) individual consumers (not businesses), regardless of location, and (b) restaurants or retail food establishments located in the same State as the farm or not more than 275 miles from the farm. Growers with a qualified exemption must comply with certain labeling requirements.

Second, FSMA requires the FDA to allocate resources to the inspection of domestic high-risk facilities that manufacture, process, pack, or hold foods and of importers according to their known safety risks. Risk factors specified by FSMA for domestic high-risk facilities include, but are not limited to, the known safety risks of the food in question, the compliance history of the facility, and the rigor and effectiveness of the facility's hazard analysis and risk-based preventive controls. Risk factors specified for importers include but are not limited to the known safety risks of the countries through which the food is transported, the compliance history of the importer, the rigor and effectiveness of the importer's activities to satisfy the requirements of the foreign supplier verification program, and the importer's participation, or lack thereof, in the voluntary qualified importer program.

Third, FSMA requires the FDA to implement more frequent inspections of both U.S. and foreign facilities. Domestic high-risk facilities must be inspected at least once during the first 5 years of the Act and at least once during each 3-year period that follows. Domestic facilities not deemed to be of high risk must be inspected at least once during the first 7 years of the Act and at least once during each 5-year period that follows. With respect to foreign facilities, FSMA requires the FDA to inspect not fewer than 600 facilities during the first year of the Act, and during each of the next 5 years, not fewer than twice the number of foreign facilities inspected in the previous year. In fiscal year (FY) 2012, the FDA and the States under contract with FDA inspected or attempted to inspect 24,462 domestic food facilities not deemed to be of high risk, and the FDA inspected 1,342 foreign food facilities and 8,023 domestic food facilities deemed to be of high risk. The FDA also re-inspected another 3,736 domestic, high-risk food facilities that it had inspected or attempted to inspect in FY 2011 (FDA, 2013b).[33] In order to work more closely with foreign regulatory authorities, the FDA has positioned staff in about a dozen foreign locations, including a post in Mexico City opened in 2009 as part of its Latin American Office (FDA, 2009). FDA does not have a similar post in Canada, but FDA has a long-standing cooperative relationship with the Canadian Government in the investigation of emergency situations, just as it does with Mexico (FDA, 2010).

Fourth, FSMA gives the FDA the authority to develop regulations that would require importers to share responsibility and be accountable for preventing food safety problems. In exercise of this authority, the FDA issued a Proposed Rule for Foreign Supplier Verification Programs (FSVP) for Importers of Food for Humans and Animals in July 2013 and revised provisions in September 2014. The proposed rule requires food importers (with some exemptions) to develop, maintain, and implement an FSVP that would include, in general, compliance status review, hazard analysis, verification activities, corrective actions, periodic reassessment of the FSVP, importer identification, and recordkeeping. In its most recent revisions, FDA has proposed a provision for required supplier verification activities that is a hybrid of two options presented in the originally proposed rule. Specifically, importers would be given the flexibility to determine appropriate verification measures based on food and supplier risks, but annual, on-site auditing of the supplier would be required when there is reason to believe that hazard would cause serious injuries or deaths. Comments on the revised provisions are being accepted until December 15, 2014 (FDA, 2014a).

One aspect of regulatory cooperation among national governments that is present in the FDA's work on FSMA is the recognition that the public and private sectors of foreign countries are important stakeholders in the U.S. regulatory system. Summary sheets for the Proposed Rule for FSVP, for instance, are available not only in English, Spanish, and French (the main languages of the NAFTA countries) but also in nine other languages. One objective of the U.S.-Mexico High-Level Regulatory Cooperation Council (HLRCC) is to intensify dialogue between the two countries on the implementation of FSMA. To this end, Mexico's Secretariat of Economy and the FDA's Latin America Regional Office held four informational workshops on FSMA in 2013, each in a different part of Mexico. In addition, the FDA's regional office conducted outreach activities on two proposed FSMA rules: the Produce Rule and the Preventive Controls for Food for Humans. These activities included information on how to offer comments on the proposed rules and how to receive further information on forthcoming FSMA implementing regulations (U.S.-Mexico HLRCC, 2013). In September 2013, the FDA held a similar outreach session with Canadian stakeholders to solicit feedback on the Produce Rule, the Preventative Controls for Food for Humans, the FSVP, and Accreditation of Third-Party Auditors/Certification Bodies to Conduct Food Safety Audits and to Issue Certifications (Dessureault, 2013).

The Search for Risk-Mitigating Tools for Intraregional Produce Trade Continues

For more than two decades, USDA's Agricultural Marketing Service has encouraged the development of risk-mitigating tools for produce trade among the NAFTA countries. This effort is guided by the belief that buyers and sellers of produce in the NAFTA region would benefit from the establishment of a North American version of the Perishable Agricultural Commodities Act (PACA) of 1930. Under PACA, which was enacted to promote fair trading practices in the U.S. fruit and vegetable industry, sellers must ship the quantity and quality of produce specified in their contracts, and buyers must accept shipments that meet contract specifications.

The first major achievement of this effort was recorded in 1999, when a group of produce and transportation companies from each NAFTA country formed the Fruit and Vegetable Dispute Resolution Corporation (DRC). The DRC describes itself as "a non-profit, membership-based organization serving the produce trade." Its main services include the provision of "harmonized standards, procedures and services … to help [members] avoid commercial disputes" and when disputes do occur, "consultation, mediation and arbitration services to resolve the issue in a timely and cost-effective manner" (Fruit and Vegetable DRC, 2014b). The DRC was created in direct response to Article 707 of NAFTA, which called for an advisory committee on private commercial disputes regarding agricultural goods.

One noteworthy innovation by the DRC is the creation of a multistep dispute resolution system that begins with preventative activities and cooperative problem-solving and then proceeds gradually to more binding measures (Fruit and Vegetable DRC, 2014a). Gómez et al. (2012) find that the DRC has facilitated produce transactions within the NAFTA region and provided an improved setting for resolving disputes in the fruit and vegetable trade—particularly in Canada, where the pre-existing licensing and arbitration system suffered from some deficiencies. Citing the corporation's administrative records, the authors emphasize that from 2000 to 2010, the DRC addressed about 1,300 disputes involving fresh fruit and vegetable trade valued at roughly $32 million.

U.S. and Canadian firms currently make up the majority of the DRC's members, while the organization's Mexican membership primarily consists of exporters rather than importers. In 2007, the DRC closed its office in Mexico, citing the country's lack of infrastructure for destination inspection and limited interest among Mexican wholesalers and retailers (Fruit and Vegetable DRC, 2007). This low level of interest may also reflect the relative size of U.S. fresh or frozen fruit and vegetable exports to Mexico, which equaled about $906 million in 2013, compared with $8.4 billion of corresponding U.S. imports from Mexico.

Even with the DRC in place, Canada still does not have a statute that effectively protects out-of- country produce suppliers from buyers that default on their payment obligations, while Canadian suppliers to U.S. firms are protected by the PACA Trust provisions. To address this difference, the U.S. and Canadian Governments continue to work on the development of "comparable approaches to financial risk mitigation tools to protect U.S. and

Canadian fruit and vegetable suppliers from buyers that default on their payment obligations"—this time within the framework of the U.S.- Canada RCC. The two governments now agree that "a single dispute resolution body approach is a critical step toward achieving comparable approaches and outcomes between Canada and the U.S. in terms of financial protection for sellers of fresh produce" (Miller and Parrott, 2014). Currently, the Canadian Government requires that produce dealers operating in Canada on an interprovincial or international basis either be a member of the DRC or be registered with the Canadian Food Inspection Agency (CFIA). In October 2014, USDA revoked the special status that Canadian produce shippers had previously enjoyed under PACA. With the revocation of this status, Canadian shippers will now be treated like shippers from any other foreign country and will need to post a bond for twice the amount of the claim to seek payment from delinquent U.S. buyers. Several media reports indicate that this action was taken because the Canadian Government has not yet instituted a risk-mitigation system similar to PACA, after years of work on this subject (Fresh Produce Alliance, 2014; Linden, 2014; *The Packer*, 2014).

New Antidumping Suspension Agreement for Tomato Imports from Mexico Takes Effect

In March 2013, the U.S. International Trade Commission suspended an antidumping duty investigation regarding tomatoes imported from Mexico, after Mexican tomato growers and nongrower exporters reached an agreement with the U.S. Department of Commerce that established a new set of floor prices for tomatoes imported from Mexico. The new agreement replaces a previous suspension agreement that was first implemented in 1996 and then revised in 2004 and 2008 (Flores and Olson, 2013b). All fresh or chilled tomatoes from Mexico are covered by the new floor prices. Fresh tomatoes are Mexico's second-leading agricultural export to the United States. In 2013, the United States imported 1.4 million metric tons of fresh tomatoes from Mexico, with a value of $1.6 billion.

The new suspension agreement differs from the previous agreement in two key respects. First, the new agreement sets different floor prices for open field/adapted-environment, controlled-environment production, and specialty tomatoes (defined in the agreement to include grape, cherry, heirloom, and ocktail tomatoes). This differentiation better reflects the structure of the tomato market and the pricing of different types of tomatoes at different times of the year. Second, the new floor prices are substantially higher than the old ones, increasing the likelihood that the floor prices have a binding effect on market prices. A simple comparison of the price floors, old and new, and the unit value of U.S. tomato imports from Mexico from November 2012 to October 2013 (table 6) suggests that while the old price floors were in many instances not binding, the new price floors may raise the price of some specialty tomatoes such as grape tomatoes. The new agreement's impact on consumer welfare is not clear, however, since one would need to compare the new price floors with a counter- factual scenario in which the antidumping investigation was allowed to run its course.

Table 6. The higher floor prices set by the new antidumping duty investigation suspension agreement for fresh tomato imports from Mexico are more likely to be binding on prices

Agreement/product	Floor prices	
	July 1 through October 22	October 23 through June 30
	Cents per pound	
2008 agreement	21.69	17.20
2013 agreement		
Open field and adapted environment	31.00	24.58
Controlled environment	41.00	32.51
Specialty, loose	51.00	35.68
Specialty, packed	59.00	46.79
Product	**Unit value of U.S. tomato imports from Mexico**	
	July-October 2013	**November 2012-June 2013**
	Cents per pound	
All tomatoes	53.13	52.701
Greenhouse tomatoes	69.62	66.75
Cherry tomatoes	66.79	63.10
Grape tomatoes	48.99	58.59
Roma tomatoes	36.48	36.11
Other tomatoes	78.11	39.13

Sources: USDA, Economic Research Service, using data from USDA/FAS (2014a) (unit values) and U.S. Department of Commerce (2013a, 2013b) (floor prices).

UNUSUALLY ABUNDANT CROPS ALTER CONDITIONS IN THE U.S.-MEXICO SUGAR AND SWEETENER MARKETS

Free trade between the United States and Mexico in sugar and high-fructose corn syrup (HFCS) started in FY 2008, following the settlement of a protracted dispute about how best to implement NAFTA's provisions for these commodities. As a result of this agreement, integration of the two countries' markets for sugar and HFCS quickly reached a high level, and bilateral free trade in these commodities increased significantly (figure 11). Imports from Mexico accounted for about 12 percent of the U.S. sugar supply during FYs 2011-13, compared with a negligible share prior to NAFTA.[34] Meanwhile, HFCS has gained greater acceptance among Mexican manufacturers of soft drinks and processed foods, although the United States still uses more HFCS on a per capita basis than does Mexico. In FY 2013, Mexico's per capita domestic sweetener use included an estimated 13 kilograms of HFCS, compared with 21 kilograms for the United States.[35]

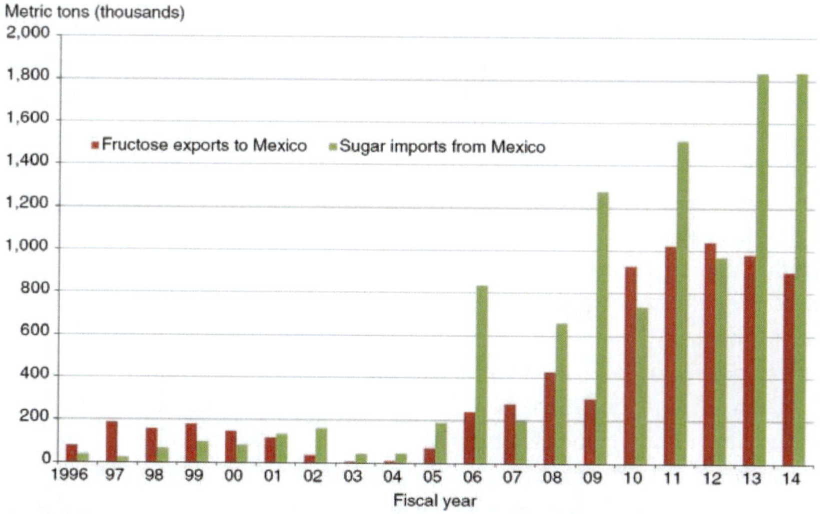

Notes: NAFTA = North American Free Trade Agreement. Fructose is defined to include high-fructose corn syrup (HFCS) and crystalline fructose.

Source: USDA, Economic Research Service, using data from USDA/FAS (2014a) (sugar imports) and Haley (2014b) (fructose exports).

Figure 11. Trade liberalization under NAFTA has led to substantial trade in sugar and fructose.

In contrast, integration of the U.S. and Canadian sugar markets remains at a low level because NAFTA exempted U.S.-Canada trade in sugar and sugar-containing products from the process of intraregional trade liberalization. Nevertheless, the U.S. and Canadian markets for processed foods are highly integrated, and there is a moderate level of trade in sugar-containing products between the two countries (app. tables 1-2). Following the establishment of free trade in sugar between the United States and Mexico, U.S. imports of sugar-containing products from both Canada and Mexico tended to level off.

The integrated U.S.-Mexico sugar and sweetener markets were shaken by much bigger than usual sugarcane and sugar beet crops during the past 2 FYs. The United States and Mexico combined produced about 15.5 million metric tons of centrifugal sugar in FY 2013 and 15.0 million metric tons in FY 2014, compared with an annual average of 12.7 million metric tons during FYs 2008-12 (table 7). This increased supply helped to lower sugar prices to levels not seen in about 5 years. The unit value of U.S. sugar imports from Mexico, for instance, dropped to $558 per metric ton in FY 2013, compared with $829 per metric ton during FYs 2010-12 and $463 per metric ton during FYs 2007-09.

Two factors account for this turn of events. First, Mexico's area harvested with sugarcane increased from 673,000 hectares to 780,000 hectares between FY 2011 and FY 2013, according to Mexican statistics (table 7). Signs of increased investments and area expansion in the Mexican sugarcane sector were observed as early as April 2010 (Flores et al., 2010), and while the U.S. sugar program uses domestic marketing allotments to influence domestic production levels, the Mexican sugar program does not contain similar controls. Second, U.S. and Mexican sugarcane growers and U.S. sugar beet growers experienced higher than average yields in FY 2013, which further boosted supply.

In response to these developments, the U.S. and Mexican Governments have taken a number of steps to reduce the supply of sugar. The U.S. Government, through the Commodity Credit Corporation (CCC), issued waivers on Re-Export licenses, purchased sugar to preempt the forfeiture of marketing loans, and then resold sugar to ethanol producers under the Feedstock Flexibility Program (FFP). While the license waivers involved no program costs, the sugar acquisitions by the CCC incurred a net cost of nearly $259 million (Haley, 2014c). The Mexican Government has encouraged its domestic sugar producers to export to markets other than the United States, and its new National Program for the Sugarcane Agroindustry for 2014-18 (PRONAC—Programa Nacional de la Agroindustria de la Caña del Azúcar) aims to foster the development of a sugarcane- based ethanol sector in Mexico (Pérez U., 2014; Mexico, Secretaría de Agricultura, Ganadería, Desarrollo Rural, Pesca, y Alimentación, 2014a, 2014b; Valverde, 2014). In FY 2013, Mexico exported about 140,000 metric tons of sugar to countries other than the United States, compared with an annual average of 20,000 metric tons during FYs 2008-12.

Table 7. U.S. and Mexican sugar production

	Fiscal year							
	2007	**2008**	**2009**	**2010**	**2011**	**2012**	**2013**	**2014**
Production of centrifugal sugar (PSD Online)								
Total, U.S. and Mexico (1,000 metric tons)	13,295	13,248	12,093	12,339	12,599	13,051	15,537	14,944
Mexico, cane sugar (1,000 metric tons)	5,633	5,852	5,260	5,115	5,495	5,351	7,393	6,890
U.S., beet sugar (1,000 metric tons)	4,543	4,283	3,823	4,150	4,226	4,446	4,607	4,559
U.S., cane sugar (1,000 metric tons)	3,119	3,113	3,010	3,074	2,878	3,254	3,537	3,495
Unit value, U.S. imports of Mexican sugar (GATS, dollars per metric ton)	462.5	446.6	471.3	755.7	835.9	873.6	558.1	517.0
Mexico, cane sugar (Sistema INFOCaña)								
Sugar production (1,000 metric tons)	5,314	5,521	4,962	4,826	5,184	5,048	6,975	n.a.
Area harvested (1,000 hectares)	675	683	663	647	673	704	780	n.a.
Yield (metric tons per hectare)	7.9	8.1	7.5	7.5	7.7	7.2	8.9	n.a.
U.S., beet sugar (Sugar and Sweetener Yearbook Tables)								
Sugar production (1,000 metric tons)	4,543	4,283	3,780	4,151	4,227	4,446	4,605	4,521
Area harvested (1,000 hectares)	528	505	407	465	468	491	487	467
Yield (metric tons per hectare)	8.6	8.5	9.3	8.9	9.0	9.1	9.5	9.7

Table 7. (Continued)

	Fiscal year							
	2007	**2008**	**2009**	**2010**	**2011**	**2012**	**2013**	**2014**
U.S., cane sugar (Sugar and Sweetener Yearbook Tables)								
Sugar production (1,000 metric tons)	3,111	3,134	3,004	3,080	2,868	3,265	3,542	3,322
Area harvested (1,000 hectares)	343	335	332	331	334	335	346	347
Yield (metric tons per hectare)	9.1	9.4	9.0	9.3	8.6	9.8	10.2	9.6

n.a. = not available.

Notes: The U.S. marketing year for sugar coincides with the fiscal year (FY) of the Federal Government, which starts on October 1 and ends on September 30. Production data from different sources may not match precisely.

Sources: USDA, Economic Research Service, using USDA/FAS (GATS, 2014a; PSD Online, 2014b); SAGARPA and CONADEZUCA (Sistema INFOCaña, 2014); and USDA/ERS (*Sugar and Sweetener Yearbook Tables*, 2014).

Some participants in the U.S. sugar industry have alleged that the Mexican Government subsidized sugar exports to the United States and that Mexican sugar exports to the United States were sold at less than fair value. In response to a petition submitted by these participants, the United States launched antidumping duty (AD) and countervailing duty (CVD) investigations in March 2014 regarding sugar imports from Mexico (USITC, 2014b). In August 2014, the U.S. Department of Commerce (USDOC) issued an affirmative preliminary decision in the CVD investigation and announced preliminary subsidy rates ranging from 2.99 percent to 17.01 percent, depending on the producer/exporter in Mexico (USDOC/ITA, 2014a). In October 2014, the USDOC announced its affirmative preliminary determination in the AD investigation and announced preliminary dumping margins ranging from 39.54 to 47.26 percent (USDOC/ITA, 2014c). However, on October 27, 2014, the USDOC announced a mutually agreeable solution suspending both investigations. The draft CVD agreement initiated by the Mexican Government includes provisions for limiting the quantity of Mexican sugar exports to the United States, while the draft AD agreement initiated by representatives of Mexican sugar exporters includes reference prices for these exports. Both draft agreements were available for comments through November 18, 2014, and may be signed no earlier than November 26, 2014.

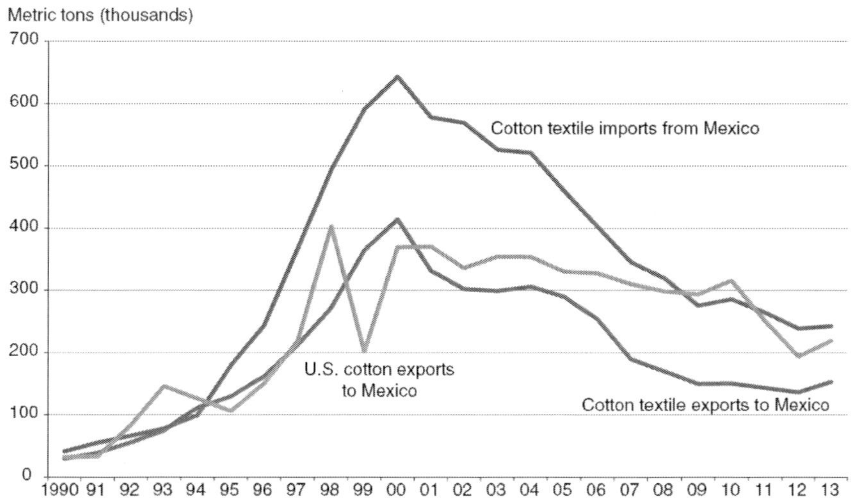

Source: USDA, Economic Research Service, using data from USDA, Economic Research Service (2014) (textile trade) and USDA/FAS (2014a) (cotton exports).

Figure 12. U.S. cotton exports to Mexico and U.S.-Mexico trade in cotton textiles declined substantially since the turn of the century.

MULTILATERAL TRADE LIBERALIZATION RESHAPES THE COTTON, TEXTILE, AND APPAREL MARKETS

North America's cotton, textile, and apparel markets became highly integrated during the first 7 years after NAFTA's implementation, as a pattern of specialization emerged in which the United States supplied raw cotton and some intermediate inputs to Mexican textile and apparel producers and Mexico exported some of its textile and apparel output to the United States. With NAFTA's liberalization of intraregional trade in cotton, textiles, and apparel, the trade flows associated with this pattern became much larger. Between 1993 and 2000, U.S. cotton exports to Mexico increased from 146,000 to 369,000 metric tons, while Mexican textile and apparel exports to the United States grew from 78,000 to 643,000 metric tons, cotton equivalent (figure 12). At the same time, U.S. textile and apparel employment continued to decline, from 1.7 million in 1993 to 1.2 million in 2000 (U.S. Department of Labor, Bureau of Labor Statistics, 1994, 2001). The U.S. textile and apparel industries had been losing jobs since the 1970s, and while trade liberalization under NAFTA helped to reinforce this trend, the integration of the U.S. and Mexican cotton, textiles, and apparel sectors and NAFTA's strict rules of origin may have helped the United States to retain jobs during the period 1994-2000 that otherwise would have relocated to other parts of the world (Zahniser and Link, 2002).

Multilateral trade liberalization under the WTO's Agreement on Textiles and Clothing, however, has exposed the integrated U.S.-Mexico cotton, textiles, and apparel sector to much greater international competition. Through this agreement, China, Vietnam, and other non-NAFTA countries gained much broader access to the North American market, effectively diminishing the preferential access that Mexico's textile and apparel sector previously had enjoyed in the United States and Canada. As a result, between 2000 and 2013, U.S. and Mexican textile and apparel production declined, U.S. textile and apparel employment dropped to 520,000 (U.S. Department of Labor, Bureau of Labor Statistics, 2014), and U.S. cotton exporters sought markets outside of Mexico. In 2013, 8 percent of U.S. cotton exports went to Mexico, compared with 25 percent in 2000.

Since the turn of the 21st century, U.S. cotton exports to Mexico and bilateral trade in cotton textiles have all declined substantially. If this trend continues, U.S. cotton exports to Mexico will reach their pre-NAFTA levels within the next decade. Honduras, a member country of the Central America-Dominican Republic-United States Free Trade Agreement (CAFTA-DR), has surpassed Mexico to become the leading destination for U.S. exports of cotton textiles, with four other CAFTA-DR countries—the Dominican Republic, El Salvador, Guatemala, and Nicaragua—in the third, fifth, seventh, and ninth positions, respectively.[36]

This suggests that some U.S. partnerships with Mexican textile and apparel manufacturers have shifted to the CAFTA-DR region. Meanwhile, China, India, Pakistan, Bangladesh, and Vietnam have each surpassed Mexico as suppliers of cotton textiles to the United States. Canada has largely shifted away from the importation and milling of cotton and is no longer among the leading exporters of cotton textiles to the United States. Canada was the 23rd largest exporter of cotton textiles to the United States; in 2000, it was the 7th largest (USDA/ERS, 2013).

A North American Approach to Deeper Integration[37]

The NAFTA governments are charting a unique course as they work to deepen the economic relationship fostered by the agreement. To date, they have elected not to establish a new organizational structure such as a customs union or a common market[38] that would take regional integration to a higher level—an approach that is different from that of the European Union (EU) and runs contrary to the counsel of some economists such as the late Bela Balassa (1961), who viewed a customs union as the next logical step after a free-trade area in the process of regional integration. Instead, the NAFTA governments are taking actions that increase the fluidity of cross-border economic activity without modifying the text of NAFTA or the free-trade area created by the agreement. Some of these actions rely upon organizational frameworks created by NAFTA, while others take place within new organizational frameworks created by the NAFTA governments over the past several years. In some instances, organizational frameworks created in conjunction with NAFTA are not currently being used on a regular basis.

From Regulatory Coordination to Regulatory Cooperation

Activities in the area of regulatory cooperation provide a clear example of the current North American approach toward deeper integration. The term "regulatory cooperation" has largely replaced the term "regulatory coordination" as a descriptor of these efforts. This change in terminology reflects the NAFTA governments' emphasis on building national regulatory systems that fit together and facilitate trade, rather than simply making adjustments to existing regulatory systems so that they do not unnecessarily impede trade. For instance, the United States and Mexico are working to develop compatible electronic Export and Import Certificate programs for plants and plant products and eventually for animals and animal products as well, while the United States and Canada have created a common nomenclature system for meat cuts.

Regulatory cooperation now relies more heavily on bilateral organizational frameworks, rather than the trilateral frameworks that are a hallmark of NAFTA's text. NAFTA established an extensive set of trilateral working groups and committees responsible for a wide variety of trade-related issues, such as the Committee on Sanitary and Phytosanitary Measures (Green et al., 2006), and it expresses the NAFTA governments' continuing commitment to the North American Plant Protection Organization (NAPPO)—a trilateral forum created in 1976 "for public and private sectors in Canada, the United States, and Mexico to collaborate in the regional protection of agricultural, forest, other plant resources, and the environment while facilitating trade" (North American Plant Protection Organization, 2011: 4). In addition, from 2005 to 2009, the NAFTA governments channeled some efforts in regulatory cooperation through the Security and Prosperity Partnership (SPP), a trilateral framework created at the highest levels of government that was intended to increase the security and enhance the prosperity of the NAFTA countries through greater cooperation and information sharing (Zahniser and Roe, 2011).

Many concrete accomplishments in regulatory cooperation involving the NAFTA countries over the past 20 years were the product of trilateral efforts, such as the coordinated campaign by all three countries to seek a harmonized approach to mitigating the risks associated with BSE and the expanded practice of sharing scientific studies and administrative evaluations among pesticide regulators and scientists in each NAFTA country (Green et al., 2006). But regulatory cooperation also took place within bilateral organizational frameworks, such as the intergovernmental Consultative Committees on Agriculture (CCAs), or through collaboration between governments at the working level. The CCAs provide a setting in which high-level agricultural and trade officials of the NAFTA governments meet on a bilateral basis to discuss various issues related to agricultural trade. The CCAs most recently met in December 2014 (U.S.-Canada and U.S.-Mexico) and August 2012 (Canada-Mexico).

While many of NAFTA's working groups and committees are still in operation, the trilateral SPP has been succeeded by several new bilateral frameworks: the U.S.-Mexico High Level Regulatory Cooperation Council, established in 2010, and the U.S.-Canada Beyond the Border (BtB) initiative and the U.S.-Canada Regulatory Cooperation Council, both established in 2011. Like the SPP, the BtB addresses mutual concerns in the areas of security and economic competitiveness, except on a bilateral (U.S.-Canada) rather than trilateral basis. By contrast, the HLRCC and RCC focus exclusively on regulatory concerns, both agricultural and nonagricultural. Relying more on bilateral frameworks is consistent with the long-standing recognition that some issues pertain to only two of the three NAFTA countries and that the regulatory priorities and capabilities of the NAFTA governments differ in ways that make it easier to cooperate on a bilateral basis. Creation of the new bilateral frameworks does not constitute an effort to abandon the trilateral working groups and committees established by NAFTA. That being said, bilateral frameworks currently seem to be the predominant approach for addressing intraregional SPS issues, as the most recent meeting of the trilateral NAFTA Committee on Sanitary and Phytosanitary Measures took place in July 2012.

Two key principles and innovative approaches to international regulatory cooperation stand out in the three bilateral frameworks. First, each country is viewed as a major stakeholder in the regulatory systems of the other country. This recognition is central, for instance, to the HLRCC's objective of intensifying the dialogue between Mexico and the United States regarding the implementation of the U.S. FDA Food Safety and Modernization Act. To this end, Mexico's Secretariat of Economy and the FDA's Latin America Regional Office in Mexico held four informational workshops on FSMA in 2013, each in a different part of Mexico. In addition, the FDA's regional office conducted outreach activities on two proposed FSMA rules: the Produce Rule and the Preventive Controls for Food for Humans. These activities included guidance on how to offer comments on the proposed rules and how to receive further information on forthcoming FSMA implementing regulations (U.S.-Mexico HLRCC, 2013).

Second, the new frameworks place strong emphasis on regulatory simplification. Several initiatives within the U.S.-Canada RCC, for instance, aim to reduce or eliminate certain inspection activities, certifications, and administrative procedures concerning food safety. As a step toward streamlining bilateral trade in meat and poultry products, the U.S. and Canadian Governments are working to identify options for simplifying or eliminating import certificates (Rathlou and Stanley, 2014), and the two governments are also taking steps so that "food safety laboratory testing conducted in one country is acceptable to regulators in both countries" (Pequignot and McGrath, 2014). The objective of regulatory simplification is also woven within several key principles of the U.S.-Mexico HLRCC's work plan.

Member Countries Gradually Revise NAFTA's Rules of Origin

The NAFTA governments also have made adjustments to the agreement's rules of origin in ways that facilitate agricultural trade. In a preferential trade agreement such as NAFTA, rules of origin determine whether a product originated from the area covered by the agreement and thus qualifies for its preferential tariff, which in NAFTA's case is usually duty-free status. Since 2003, the NAFTA governments have made incremental changes to the accord's rules of origin through the NAFTA Working Group on Rules of Origin (WGRO). A few of these changes apply directly to agriculture. For instance, one modification allows the regional content of certain cranberry juice mixtures to be determined by transaction value or net cost, rather than volume (Zahniser et al., 2009), while another modification allows for certain crushed or ground spices produced in the NAFTA region to qualify for duty-free status even when they were obtained from spices (not crushed or ground) sourced outside the NAFTA region (USITC, 2009). During the latter half of 2013, the USITC received comments on a new round of proposed changes to NAFTA's rules of origin, including one that would affect miscellaneous edible preparations in HS Code 2103.90 (Executive Office of the President of the United States, 2013).

Immigration Reform Intersects with Regional Integration

Regional integration is also affected by policy responses to issues that are largely separate from NAFTA, such as national immigration laws. As part of NAFTA, each member country agreed to allow the temporary entry of people from other member countries if they were business persons, traders, investors, or members of certain professions, but hired farm labor is not one of these professions. Nevertheless, certain labor-intensive sectors of U.S. agriculture, such as horticultural production, rely heavily on foreign-born workers, and many of these workers lack the immigration status needed to work legally in the United States. According to the U.S. Department of Labor's National Agricultural Workers Survey (NAWS), roughly half of the hired labor force in U.S. crop agriculture is believed to be unauthorized, with the vast majority of these unauthorized workers coming from Mexico (Hertz, 2013).

The Federal Government already operates a program—the H-2A Temporary Agricultural Worker Program—that allows agricultural employers to hire foreign-born farmworkers who are not permanent residents of the United States on a temporary or seasonal basis. Its participation levels are small relative to the number of unauthorized immigrants working in U.S. agriculture.

In FY 2013, the U.S. Department of Labor (USDOL) certified 98,813 positions for the program (USDOL/ETA, 2013: p. 30). By comparison, the number of hired laborers employed by U.S. agriculture in 2013 ranged from 596,000 in January to 906,000 in July, according to quarterly estimates (USDA/NASS, 2014a). While there are no annual limits to the number of H-2A workers who may enter the country, other aspects of the program limit its use.

Since the program is only for temporary or seasonal workers, dairy, livestock, and nursery operations are largely precluded from participating. In addition, some prospective employers may be discouraged by the application process and other requirements of the program, including the requirement to pay H-2A workers the highest of the Federal or State minimum wage, the prevailing hourly or piece rate, the agreed-upon collective bargaining rate, or the adverse effect wage rate (AEWR), as determined by USDOL.

Recent sessions of the U.S. Congress have considered proposals to modify U.S. immigration law in ways that would affect the extent to which the U.S. and Mexican markets for hired farm labor are integrated. One proposal would create a mechanism by which many of the sector's unauthorized workers and their families could apply for at first temporary and eventually permanent legal residency in the United States. One expert assessment of this proposal's potential implications for California (Martin, 2013) concludes that such legalizations would greatly increase the proportion of the sector's current workforce that is legally authorized to work in the United States. Such a change could benefit agricultural employers by reducing their risk of being fined for immigration law violations and/or seeing their labor supply disrupted by immigration enforcement activities.

Another proposal would replace the H-2A program with a new agricultural guestworker program. Under the proposed program, employers would register with USDA's Farm Service Agency (FSA) to become "Designated Agricultural Employers." This process would involve paying a fee, documenting engagement in agriculture, and estimating how many workers would be needed.

Any agricultural employer would have access to the program for both year-round and seasonal labor needs. As with the H-2A Program, the employer would be required to advertise the job with the State workforce agency, and preference would be given to applicants who are U.S. citizens or permanent residents. Within 45 days of when workers are needed, the employer would be required to file a petition with the U.S. Department of Homeland Security (DHS) attesting how many workers are needed, when they are needed, specifics of their contracts, and evidence of the State workforce advertisement. DHS would be required to grant the request for guestworkers within 7 working days unless the petition was found to be incomplete or inaccurate.

Once the employee completes the initial job contract, she or he would become an "at-will" worker with permission to work for any designated agricultural employer.

The employee would be allowed to stay in the United States for up to 3 years and would be eligible for a 3-year extension but would not be allowed to have more than a 2-month break in employment. The program's at-will component would give workers the flexibility desired by labor advocates. At-will workers are the same as any authorized worker, except that they can only work in agriculture. They do not sign contracts unless they want to. If they feel they are treated poorly, they are free to move on to another employer. When the visa expires, workers must return home for at least 3 months before starting the process over, if they desire. Family members (spouse and children) of the employee are not allowed to accompany the worker during his or her term of employment. Employers pay transportation costs, and must provide either on-site housing or housing vouchers under certain conditions. For the first 4 years, the program would have an annual cap of 112,333 workers spread out evenly over four quarters. In later years, the Secretary of Agriculture would be responsible for establishing the annual cap.

Zahniser et al. (2012) use an economic simulation model to examine the effects of a 156,000-person increase in the employment of temporary nonimmigrant agricultural workers, such as those now participating in the H-2A Program. Findings from this study suggest that an expanded agricultural guestworker program would lead to longrun increases in U.S. agricultural output and exports.

The increases in the modeling results are generally larger in labor-intensive sectors, such as fruit, tree nuts, vegetables, and nursery products. By year 15 of the simulation, these four sectors experience a 1.1- to 2.0-percent increase in output and a 1.7- to 3.2-percent increase in exports, relative to the model's base forecast.

Less labor-intensive sectors, such as grains, oilseeds, and livestock production, tend to have smaller increases, ranging from 0.1 to 1.5 percent for output and from 0.2 to 2.6 percent for exports.

EXTENDING FREE TRADE TO NEW MARKETS

In addition to working to deepen regional integration, the NAFTA countries are seeking more open trading relations with non-NAFTA countries as a means of cultivating new markets for their agricultural and nonagricultural products. Currently, all three NAFTA governments are negotiating additional FTAs with countries in other parts of the world—building upon their extensive network of FTAs with trade partners in Latin America, the Caribbean, Asia, Europe, Africa, and the Middle East. As of October 2014, the NAFTA countries had implemented a total of 30 FTAs with 53 countries outside the NAFTA region (table 8).

The tariff preferences provided by these additional FTAs are generally similar to those that Canada, Mexico, and the United States extend to each other through NAFTA—including duty-free access for a wide range of agricultural products. Thus, these FTAs are a possible source of preference erosion with respect to agricultural trade among the NAFTA countries. A cursory look at agricultural import data, however, suggests that such preference erosion has not been a widespread challenge, as the NAFTA countries' shares in each other's total agricultural imports have changed little over the past decade (table 9).

Several ongoing trade negotiations involving the NAFTA countries are "super-regional"—meaning that they engage trade partners in more than one region of the world and would potentially cover a larger amount of economic activity than a traditional bilateral or regional trade agreement such as NAFTA. One super-regional initiative underway is the Trans-Pacific Partnership (TPP), which aspires to foster greater economic integration among 12 countries in the Pacific Rim: Australia, Brunei Darussalam, Chile, Japan, Malaysia, New Zealand, Peru, Singapore, Vietnam, and the 3 NAFTA partners. The TPP is important for many reasons, including its objective to establish comprehensive market access among the member countries and its involvement of major agricultural exporting and importing countries. Other super-regional initiatives involving the NAFTA countries include the agreement-in-principle for the Canada-EU Comprehensive Economic and Trade Agreement (CETA), the Transatlantic Trade and Investment Partnership (TTIP) negotiations between the United States and EU, and a trade agreement signed in August 2013 under the rubric of the Alianza del Pacífico, a regional integration initiative involving Mexico, Chile, Colombia, and Peru.

Table 8. The NAFTA countries already have multiple FTAs with the rest of the world

Central America and the Caribbean							
	Costa Rica	**El Salvador**	**Guatemala**	**Honduras**	**Nicaragua**	**Dominican Republic**	**Panama**
U.S.	2009	2006	2006	2006	2006	2007	2012
Mexico	1995, 2013	2001, 2012	2001, 2013	2001, 2013	1998, 2012	--	Pending*
Canada	2002	--	--	Pending*	--	--	2013
South America							
	Colombia	**Bolivia**	**Chile**	**Uruguay**	**Peru**		
U.S.	2012	--	2005, TPP	--	2009, TPP		
Mexico	1994, 2011, AP	1995, 2010	1999, AP, TPP	2004	2012, AP, TPP		
Canada	2011	--	1997, TPP	--	2009, TPP		
Asia							
	Singapore	**Australia**	**Japan**	**South Korea**	**Malaysia**	**New Zealand**	**Vietnam**
U.S.	2004, TPP	2005, TPP	TPP	2012	TPP	TPP	TPP
Mexico	TPP	TPP	2005, TPP	--	TPP	TPP	TPP
Canada	TPP	TPP	TPP	--	TPP	TPP	TPP

Europe, Africa, and Middle East								
	Israel	European Union	European Free Trade Association	Jordan	Bahrain	Morocco	Oman	BruneiDarus-salam
U.S.	1985	TTIP	--	2001	2006	2006	2009	TPP
Mexico	2000	2000	2001	--	--	--	--	TPP
Canada	1997	Pending*	2009	2012	--	--	--	TPP

Notes: Years indicate when the relevant FTA was implemented. TPP = Trans-Pacific Partnership, TTIP = Transatlantic Trade and Investment Partnership, and AP = Alianza del Pacífico. European Free Trade Association encompasses Iceland, Liechtenstein, Norway, and Switzerland. European Union encompasses Austria, Belgium, Bulgaria, Croatia, Cyprus, Czech Republic, Denmark, Estonia, Finland, France, Germany, Greece, Hungary, Ireland, Italy, Latvia, Lithuania, Luxemburg, Malta, Netherlands, Poland, Portugal, Romania, Slovakia, Slovenia, Spain, Sweden, and United Kingdom.

* Mexico concluded negotiations of an FTA with Panama in February 2014; Canada reached an agreement-in-principle with the European Union (CETA) in October 2013 and signed an FTA with Honduras in November 2013. These agreements need to be approved by the legislative bodies of the participating countries before entering into force.

Source: Table presented in Zahniser and Herrera Moreno (2014), using data from Organization of American States (2014).

Mexico's recent trade negotiations have provided it with the opportunity to consolidate several of its existing FTAs and broaden market access for agricultural and nonagricultural products. For example, the recent trade agreement forged by the Alianza del Pacífico consolidates the bilateral FTAs that Chile, Colombia, Mexico, and Peru had with each other while providing for a transition to duty-free trade in almost all agricultural products, with sugar and sugar-containing products being notable exceptions. Similarly, the Mexico-Central America Free Trade Agreement replaces Mexico's bilateral FTAs with Costa Rica and with Nicaragua and its regional FTA with El Salvador, Guatemala, and Honduras. The new Mexico-Central America agreement features additional preferential market access for some sensitive items like sugar and dairy products as well as a consolidated set of rules of origin that applies to all member countries (México, Secretaría de Economía, 2011c: 4-5). Although NAFTA includes a mechanism for the accession of new member countries, that mechanism has never been used.

Table 9. NAFTA countries' shares of each other's total agricultural imports have changed little over the past decade

Exporter	United States		Canada		Mexico	
	2001-03	2011-13	2001-03	2011-13	2001-03	2011-13
	Percent					
Total, NAFTA countries	37	36	63	63	81	80
United States	--	--	61	59	74	72
Canada	24	20	--	--	7	8
Mexico	13	16	2	4	--	--
Total, non-NAFTA countries	63	64	37	37	19	20

NAFTA = North American Free Trade Agreement.

Note: For Canada and Mexico, agricultural imports are defined as Chapters 1-24 in the Harmonized System.

Sources: USDA, Economic Research Service, using USDA/FAS (2014a), and Mexico, Secretaría de Economía, and Statistics Canada, both as cited by Global Trade Information Service (2014).

The interest of the NAFTA countries in markets outside the NAFTA region reflects both the tremendous progress that has been made by removing trade barriers through NAFTA and other FTAs and the degree to which changes in the world's demographics and economics have diminished the relative importance of the NAFTA region. According to the U.S. Census Bureau's *International Database*, the world's population is projected to grow from 7.2 billion to 8.6 billion over the next 20 years (2014-34), with 94 percent of the total increase corresponding to non-NAFTA countries. Two continents are expected to account for a combined 89 percent of the projected increase: (1) Asia (excluding the Near East), due to the large size of its current population, and (2) Africa, due to its fast rate of projected population growth.[39]

In addition, several Asian countries are projected to have compound annual growth rates in real per capita income in excess of 5 percent over the next 15 years (2015-30), including Bhutan, Burma, Cambodia, China, India, Laos, Sri Lanka, and TPP partner Vietnam. Five percent is well above the average rates projected for the United States (1.87 percent), Canada (1.76 percent), and Mexico (3.13 percent) (USDA/ERS, 2014). For these reasons, agricultural producers in North America should be expected to increase their efforts to serve markets outside the NAFTA region. This trend is exemplified by the recent attention paid by pork and beef exporters in each NAFTA country to Asian markets and the efforts of each NAFTA country to negotiate additional trade agreements with non-NAFTA countries.

Still, the projections support expectations that the NAFTA region will also be a growing market. Among the NAFTA countries, the United States is expected to have the largest increase in population over the next two decades by virtue of the size of its current population and its projected rate of population growth relative to that of Canada and Mexico (figure 13). Between 2014 and 2034, the region's population is projected to increase by about 76 million—49 million in the United States, 23 million in Mexico, and 4 million in Canada. This anticipated population growth heightens the attractiveness of the U.S. market, particularly to domestic producers and to Canadian and Mexican producers, who are proximate and enjoy duty-free access because of NAFTA.

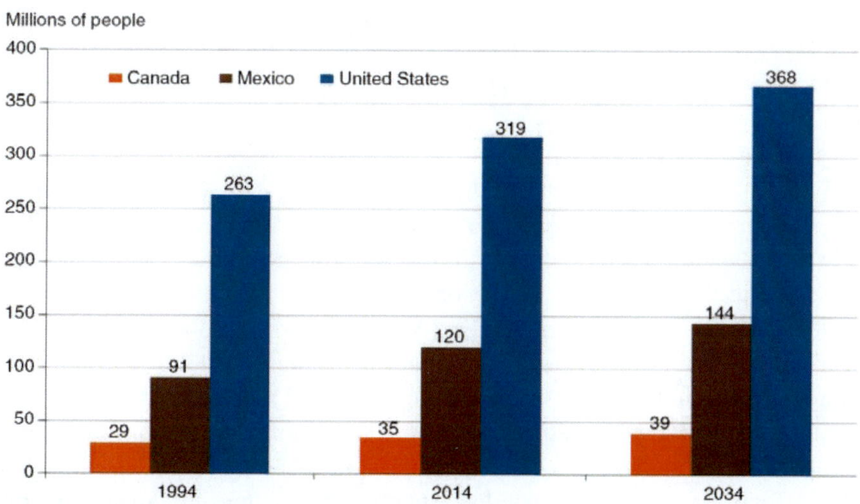

NAFTA = North American Free Trade Agreement.

Source: USDA, Economic Research Service, using data from U.S. Department of Commerce, Bureau of the Census (2013).

Figure 13. The total population of the NAFTA region is projected to increase by 76 million over the next 20 years.

CONCLUSION

The 20th anniversary of NAFTA provides testimony to the lasting value of agricultural trade liberalization to the North American economy. By removing thousands of tariffs, quotas, import licensing requirements, and other policy measures that formerly distorted agricultural trade and FDI among the United States, Canada, and Mexico, NAFTA facilitated a large increase in cross-border economic activity in the agricultural and processed food sectors. While the patterns of specialization in intraregional agricultural trade reflect the resource endowments, climatological conditions, and accumulated skills and abilities of the three NAFTA countries, the active participation of producers, intermediaries, and consumers from each member country in the larger and far more integrated continental agricultural market fostered by NAFTA is a function of the agreement's scope and comprehensiveness. To date, few other trade agreements have created a free-trade area that encompasses an economy as large as that formed by the United States, Canada, and Mexico and institutes tariff- and quota-free intraregional trade for virtually all agricultural products.

The ongoing TPP and TTIP negotiations provide their respective participants with opportunities to establish new trade agreements that could surpass NAFTA in this regard.

With the passage of time, the specifics of NAFTA's agricultural provisions are likely to fade from most people's memories, even for those who study the agricultural sector closely. In the long run, NAFTA's significance in the history of the North American economy is likely to be the closing of one chapter in which tariffs, quotas, and other barriers obstruct potential opportunities for intra-regional trade and investment and the opening of another chapter in which the member countries work more closely together to develop such economic relationships and to seek similar relationships with other parts of the world.

The first few pages of that new chapter tell of the implementation of NAFTA, and the rest of the chapter, of course, remains to be written.

Appendix table 1. Selected U.S. agricultural exports to Canada, 1991-93 versus 2011-1

	Value			Volume			Unit Value		
	Average annual		Change	Average annual		Change	For period		Change
	1991 -93	2011 -13		1991 -93	2011 -13		1991 -93	2011 -13	
	U.S. dollars (millions)		*Percent*	*Metric tons (thousands)*		*Percent*	*U.S. dollars per kilogram*		*Percent*
Total	4,954	20,332	310	--	--	--	--	--	--
Animals and animal products	909	3,779	316	--	--	--	--	--	--
Beef and veal	363	1,100	203	87	168	94	4.19	6.53	56
Pork	29	787	2,589	9	204	2,075	3.14	3.86	23
Chickens, fresh or frozen	85	360	323	42	140	231	2.03	2.58	27
Poultry meats, prepared or preserved	54	182	240	12	44	256	4.33	4.13	-5
Sausage, other than chicken and turkey	23	161	596	5	34	561	4.56	4.79	5
Preparations for infant use, retail sale	4	117	2,590	1	25	2,254	4.05	4.72	17
Mink furskins, raw, whole[5]	17	108	549	1,633	2,478	52	10.14	43.38	328
Puddings ready for immediate consumption	4	86	2,103	3	55	1,995	1.49	1.57	5
Eggs	31	88	184	--	--	--	--	--	--
Whey, fluid or dried	10	83	721	--	--	--	--	--	--
Cheese	10	66	576	2	13	457	4.11	4.99	21
Milk albumin, including concentrates of two or more whey proteins	--	52	--	--	5	--	--	9.82	--
Cattle and calves[1]	36	33	-8	71	63	-12	506.51	528.46	4
Other	242	555	129	--	--	--	--	--	--

Appendix table 1. (Continued)

	Value			Volume			Unit Value		
	Average annual		Change	Average annual		Change	For period		Change
	1991-93	2011-13		1991-93	2011-13		1991-93	2011-13	
	U.S. dollars (millions)		*Percent*	*Metric tons (thousands)*		*Percent*	*U.S. dollars per kilogram*		*Percent*
Grains and feeds	759	3,647	380	1,658	3,885	134	0.47	0.94	98
Dog or cat food, retail sale	146	568	290	142	274	93	1.04	2.08	100
Pastry, cake, bread, and pudding	101	473	367	62	163	164	1.65	2.91	76
Prepared food from swelling or roasting of cereal or cereal products	36	317	789	19	120	544	1.91	2.64	38
Mixes and doughs	31	234	650	27	127	367	1.15	1.83	59
Mixed feeds or mixed feed ingredients, excluding pet food	84	202	141	145	176	21	0.59	1.15	94
Stuffed, canned, and other prepared pasta	30	184	521	14	81	482	2.12	2.26	7
Other bread, pastry, cake, biscuits, and bakery wares, excluding pizza and quiche	8	176	1,975	5	52	1,057	1.88	3.37	79
Corn	60	171	187	600	671	12	0.10	0.26	153
Rice	56	164	193	142	227	60	0.39	0.72	83
Cookies, waffles, and wafers	48	161	233	25	62	150	1.64	2.58	57
Brewing or distilling dregs and waste	2	150	8,085	14	605	4,119	0.13	0.25	93
Corn chips and similar crisp snack foods	11	132	1,113	6	41	547	1.76	3.22	83
Cereals (other than corn) or worked grains (except flour, groats, and meal), not bulgur wheat, not frozen	--	95	--	--	54	--	--	1.78	--

	Value			Volume			Unit Value		
	Average annual		Change	Average annual		Change	For period		Change
	1991-93	2011-13		1991-93	2011-13		1991-93	2011-13	
	U.S. dollars (millions)		*Percent*	*Metric tons (thousands)*		*Percent*	*U.S. dollars per kilogram*		*Percent*
Pizza and quiche	11	86	659	3	24	604	3.28	3.53	8
Pasta, uncooked, not containing egg[2]	17	77	354	15	63	310	1.11	1.23	11
Wheat flour	3	58	1,912	10	106	928	0.27	0.55	99
Other	115	399	247	--	--	--	--	--	--
Fruits and preparations, excl. juice	711	2,192	208	872	1,272	46	0.82	1.72	110
Strawberries, fresh	51	322	534	36	115	221	1.41	2.80	98
Grapes, fresh	117	212	81	112	97	-14	1.05	2.19	110
Apples, fresh	58	191	230	76	134	76	0.76	1.42	87
Cherries, fresh	15	142	851	7	30	314	2.14	4.79	124
Oranges, fresh or dried	80	139	73	155	153	-1	0.55	0.91	65
Raspberries, blackberries, mulberries, and loganberries, fresh	4	136	3,104	7	21	183	0.58	6.57	1,031
Blueberries, fresh	10	114	1,068	8	32	302	1.25	3.62	191
Watermelons, fresh	25	83	227	78	151	94	0.37	0.55	48
Peaches, fresh	46	76	66	50	42	-15	0.93	1.81	95
Pears, fresh	26	54	112	37	45	24	0.70	1.20	70
Other	279	722	159	--	--	--	--	--	--
Fruit juices[3]	156	544	248	267	512	92	0.59	1.06	80
Orange juice[3]	83	289	249	155	347	124	0.54	0.83	55

Appendix table 1. (Continued)

	Value			Volume			Unit Value		Change
	Average annual		Change	Average annual		Change	For period		
	1991-93	2011-13		1991-93	2011-13		1991-93	2011-13	
	U.S. dollars (millions)		*Percent*	*Metric tons (thousands)*		*Percent*	*U.S. dollars per kilogram*		*Percent*
Mixtures of fruit juices, unfermented, not fortified with vitamins or minerals	8	73	844	11	46	337	0.75	1.60	114
Other	66	181	175	--	--	--	--	--	--
Wine[4]	42	388	827	32	57	79	1.28	6.80	429
Nuts and preparations	129	708	448	72	206	186	1.78	3.43	93
Almonds, fresh or dried	30	186	520	9	32	256	3.37	5.83	73
Peanuts, shelled	38	89	136	43	70	63	0.89	1.27	43
Walnuts, fresh or dried	12	79	538	4	9	114	2.86	8.52	198
Popcorn, microwaveable	--	62	--	--	31	--	--	1.99	--
Pecans, fresh or dried	19	54	177	3	4	28	5.57	12.10	117
Other	30	238	705	--	--	--	--	--	--
Vegetables and preparations	918	2,737	198	--	--	--	--	--	--
Lettuce, fresh	109	423	286	254	297	17	0.43	1.42	230
Potatoes, fresh[4]	62	119	92	179	264	47	0.36	0.45	27
Potatoes, frozen	1	84	6,061	1	44	3,075	0.99	1.91	94
Potato chips	24	74	206	10	17	75	2.48	4.35	75
Tomato sauces, other than ketchup	36	149	319	35	149	331	0.90	1.00	11
Other sauces and preparations	25	133	426	17	53	220	1.51	2.49	64

	Value			Volume			Unit Value		
	Average annual		Change	Average annual		Change	For period		Change
	1991-93	2011-13		1991-93	2011-13		1991-93	2011-13	
	U.S. dollars (millions)		*Percent*	*Metric tons (thousands)*		*Percent*	*U.S. dollars per kilogram*		*Percent*
Tomatoes, fresh	114	123	8	137	89	-35	0.83	1.37	65
Carrots, fresh	26	114	348	71	99	39	0.36	1.16	222
Onions and shallots, fresh	42	106	149	103	153	48	0.41	0.69	68
Cauliflower, fresh	32	94	198	44	88	99	0.72	1.08	50
Spinach, fresh or chilled	9	85	809	12	28	131	0.76	3.00	294
Peppers, fresh	45	81	82	69	55	-20	0.68	1.48	120
Broccoli, fresh	41	76	84	72	65	-10	0.57	1.16	104
Celery, fresh	36	65	81	96	93	-3	0.37	0.70	87
Kohlrabi, fresh or chilled	5	57	1,113	7	39	491	0.70	1.45	105
Other	311	955	207	--	--	--	--	--	--
Oilseeds and products	322	1,577	390	961	2,027	111	0.33	0.78	133
Soybean meal	151	439	190	625	1,005	61	0.24	0.44	80
Soybeans	37	111	197	154	227	48	0.24	0.49	105
Soybean oil	8	43	459	15	30	103	0.53	1.46	177
Rapeseed	8	97	1,172	29	122	320	0.26	0.79	204
Rapeseed oil	2	133	7,697	3	119	4,572	0.74	1.12	52
Protein substances	16	119	638	6	17	178	2.58	6.89	167
Vegetable fats and oils and their fractions, hydrogenated, inter-esterified, reesterified, or elaidinized	6	85	1,354	5	52	934	1.16	1.62	39

Appendix table 1. (Continued)

	Value			Volume			Unit Value		
	Average annual		Change	Average annual		Change	For period		Change
	1991-93	2011-13		1991-93	2011-13		1991-93	2011-13	
	U.S. dollars (millions)		*Percent*	*Metric tons (thousands)*		*Percent*	*U.S. dollars per kilogram*		*Percent*
Other animal or vegetable fats and oils, not elsewhere specified	6	66	1,069	4	29	572	1.32	2.30	74
Baking or frying fats, made from artificial mixtures of products in headings 1501 to 1515, not containing 5 percent or more by weight of soybean oil or any fraction thereof	2	59	2,885	2	68	2,899	0.88	0.88	-0
Other	87	425	390	--	--	--	--	--	--
Cotton, excluding linters	61	2	-97	37	1	-98	1.62	2.47	52
Essential oils	48	345	611	4	26	557	11.48	13.15	15
Mixtures of odoriferous substances for use in food and beverage industry	33	309	826	3	23	737	12.28	13.66	11
Other	15	35	134	--	--	--	--	--	--
Seeds, field and garden	67	271	306	39	110	184	1.73	2.47	43
Corn seed, excluding sweet corn seed	10	124	1,140	8	26	221	1.25	4.82	286
Other	57	147	159	--	--	--	--	--	--

	Value			Volume			Unit Value		
	Average annual		Change	Average annual		Change	For period		Change
	1991 -93	2011 -13		1991 -93	2011 -13		1991 -93	2011 -13	
	U.S. dollars (millions)		*Percent*	*Metric tons (thousands)*		*Percent*	*U.S. dollars per kilogram*		*Percent*
Sugar and tropical products	396	2,029	413	--	--	--	--	--	--
Coffee, roasted, not decaffeinated	44	580	1,206	9	70	700	5.14	8.31	62
Sugar confections and sweetmeats without cocoa	61	222	262	30	71	139	2.07	3.13	51
Cocoa preparations in bulk form	18	133	629	8	48	475	2.22	2.79	26
Food preparations containing cocoa other than confectionery, put up for retail sale	2	121	5,569	*	27	5,365	1.43	4.45	211
Tea, including herbal tea	22	108	389	4	19	337	5.20	5.64	9
Confectionery and food preparations containing cocoa, not elsewhere specified	51	94	84	17	19	14	2.38	4.86	104
Glucose or glucose syrup	24	97	299	63	189	202	0.39	0.51	31
Fructose syrup, containing more than 50 percent by weight of fructose, not elsewhere specified	23	62	176	71	150	109	0.32	0.42	32
Chocolate and other food preparations containing cocoa, confectionery, in blocks, slabs, or bars weighing 2 kilograms or less, filled	10	71	643	3	15	342	1.54	4.79	211

Appendix table 1. (Continued)

	Value			Volume			Unit Value		
	Average annual		Change	Average annual		Change	For period		Change
	1991-93	2011-13		1991-93	2011-13		1991-93	2011-13	
	U.S. dollars (millions)		*Percent*	*Metric tons (thousands)*		*Percent*	*U.S. dollars per kilogram*		*Percent*
Confectionery containing synthetic sweetening agents instead of sugar	1	58	5,108	*	7	2,664	4.61	8.69	88
Spices	18	54	204	8	24	203	2.26	2.27	0
Other	121	429	255	--	--	--	--	--	--
Other horticultural products	173	1,183	586	--	--	--	--	--	--
Soups, broths, and other preparations, not based on fish or other seafood, not dried	5	94	1,714	3	42	1,207	1.64	2.23	36
Mixed condiments and mixed seasonings	13	79	486	4	24	479	2.65	3.30	24
Starches, excluding wheat and corn starch	22	73	235	36	72	100	0.63	1.02	62
Enzymes or prepared enzymes not elsewhere specified or indicated; excludes rennet and Penicillin G amidase	--	55	--	--	6	--	--	8.88	--
Other	132	881	568	--	--	--	--	--	--
Nursery and greenhouse products	110	203	86	--	--	--	--	--	--
Beverages excluding juices	109	703	542	--	--	--	--	--	--
Nonalcoholic beverages other than carbonated soft drinks, nonalcoholic beer, and cider	24	278	1,035	29	203	606	0.85	1.37	61

	Value			Volume			Unit Value		
	Average annual		Change	Average annual		Change	For period		Change
	1991-93	2011-13		1991-93	2011-13		1991-93	2011-13	
	U.S. dollars (millions)		*Percent*	*Metric tons (thousands)*		*Percent*	*U.S. dollars per kilogram*		*Percent*
Preparations for the manufacture of beverages	44	183	319	8	17	114	5.34	10.52	97
Beer made from malt[3]	20	145	621	39	85	120	0.57	1.70	198
Carbonated soft drinks	9	79	755	16	108	581	0.62	0.73	17
Other	12	18	50	--	--	--	--	--	--
Other	45	25	-44	--	--	--	--	--	--

-- = not applicable.

[1] Volume is measured in thousands of head, and unit value is measured in dollars per head.

[2] Excludes canned pasta and stuffed pasta.

[3] Volume is measured in millions of liters, and unit value is measured in dollars per liter.

[4] Excludes seed potatoes.

[5] Volume is measured in thousands of pelts, and unit value is measured in dollars per pelt.

[*] Less than 500 metric tons.

Source: Prepared by USDA Economic Research Service, using data from U.S. Department of Commerce, Bureau of the Census, *Foreign Trade Statistics*, as presented by USDA/FAS (2014a).

Appendix table 2. Selected U.S. agricultural imports from Canada, 1991-93 versus 2011-13

	Value			Volume			Unit Value		
	1991 -93	**2011 -13**	**Change**	**1991 -93**	**2011 -13**	**Change**	**1991 -93**	**2011 -13**	**Change**
	U.S. dollars (millions)		*Percent*	*Metric tons (thousands)*		*Percent*	*U.S. dollars per kilogram*		*Percent*
Total	4,044	20,298	402	--	--	--	--	--	--
Animals and animal products	1,784	4,463	150	--	--	--	--	--	--
Cattle and calves[1]	802	1,055	32	1,127	848	-25	706.63	1,243.62	76
Pork	368	950	158	177	289	63	2.08	3.29	58
Beef and veal	283	826	192	121	201	66	2.34	4.12	76
Beef variety meats	15	77	411	8	14	87	1.95	5.33	173
Swine[1]	82	341	315	854	5,470	541	65.47	62.34	-5
Confectionery (including gum) containing synthetic sweetening agents instead of sugar	--	133	--	--	16	--	--	8.39	--
Food preparations of flour, starch, and dairy, not elsewhere specified	2	121	6,221	2	41	2,134	1.05	2.97	183
Mink furskins[2]	22	118	435	1,071	1,916	79	20.57	61.38	198
Chicken, fresh or frozen	1	114	11,130	1	37	5,489	1.52	3.09	103
Chicken sausages and similar products	--	89	--	--	20	--	--	4.46	--
Bovine hides and skins, whole[3]	65	43	-34	1,620	667	-59	40.05	64.14	60
Other	143	598	317	--	--	--	--	--	--
Grains and feeds	759	4,990	557	--	--	--	--	--	--
Wheat, excluding seed	154	813	428	1,268	2,514	98	0.12	0.32	167
Bread, pastry, cakes, biscuits, and puddings	146	756	417	77	231	198	2.00	3.27	64

	Value			Volume			Unit Value		
	1991-93	2011-13	Change	1991-93	2011-13	Change	1991-93	2011-13	Change
	U.S. dollars (millions)		*Percent*	*Metric tons (thousands)*		*Percent*	*U.S. dollars per kilogram*		*Percent*
Sweet biscuits, waffles, and wafers, not frozen	17	454	2,508	8	108	1,196	2.19	4.22	92
Sweet biscuits, waffles, and wafers, frozen	*	157	93,956	*	53	77,062	3.37	2.95	-12
Oats, unmilled	54	379	604	576	1,501	161	0.10	0.25	157
Grains, rollled or flaked, of oats	1	73	5,914	4	108	2,603	0.30	0.68	126
Groats and meal of oats	3	70	2,437	11	143	1,229	0.26	0.49	89
Mixes and doughs	14	270	1,812	12	138	1,041	1.22	1.95	60
Corn, unmilled	27	234	753	284	838	195	0.10	0.28	188
Dog or cat food, retail sale	46	206	347	67	84	27	0.69	2.45	254
Prepared food from swelling or roasting cereal flakes or products	48	205	331	27	81	198	1.76	2.54	44
Malt, not roasted	3	178	5,854	13	278	2,082	0.24	0.64	171
Mixed feeds or mixed feed ingredients, excluding bird feed and pet food	44	121	177	166	155	-6	0.26	0.78	198
Pasta and noodles[4]	12	116	849	12	45	259	0.99	2.61	163
Barley, unmilled	46	109	137	474	354	-25	0.10	0.31	212
Cereals other than corn, grain form, precooked or otherwise prepared, not frozen	*	104	21,057	*	38	11,998	1.39	2.71	95
Wheat or meslin flour	13	84	560	46	120	162	0.11	0.70	532
Brewing or distilling dregs and waste	7	82	990	58	378	550	0.13	0.22	67

Appendix table 2. (Continued)

	Value			Volume			Unit Value		
	1991 -93	2011 -13	Change	1991 -93	2011 -13	Change	1991 -93	2011 -13	Change
	U.S. dollars (millions)		*Percent*	*Metric tons (thousands)*		*Percent*	*U.S. dollars per kilogram*		*Percent*
Stuffed, canned, or other prepared pasta	7	53	718	6	12	109	1.27	4.58	261
Other	116	524	351	--	--	--	--	--	--
Fruits and preparations, excluding juice	71	533	652	100	224	125	0.72	2.38	229
Blueberries, frozen	10	124	1,203	6	36	555	1.72	3.41	99
Blueberries, fresh	10	93	813	9	26	202	1.17	3.56	204
Cranberries, fresh	12	65	464	17	51	203	0.70	1.29	85
Other	40	251	534	--	--	--	--	--	--
Fruit juices[4]	10	73	644	16	76	375	0.62	0.96	57
Nuts	14	72	399	10	19	99	1.49	3.73	150
Vegetables and preparations	195	2,292	1,073	--	--	--	--	--	--
Potatoes, frozen	54	717	1,238	99	741	650	0.54	0.97	79
Potatoes, fresh[5]	33	150	357	189	412	118	0.17	0.37	117
Tomatoes, fresh	5	296	5,317	4	140	3,235	1.36	2.11	55
Peppers, fresh	5	229	4,267	3	96	3,624	2.10	2.39	14
Cucumbers, fresh	3	137	3,893	4	91	2,364	0.94	1.51	61
Mushrooms, fresh or chilled	3	105	3,548	2	30	1,642	1.68	3.47	107
Sauces and preparations, not elsewhere specified	--	89	--	--	29	--	--	3.06	--
Other	92	568	519	--	--	--	--	--	--

	Value			Volume			Unit Value		
	1991-93	2011-13	Change	1991-93	2011-13	Change	1991-93	2011-13	Change
	U.S. dollars (millions)		*Percent*	*Metric tons (thousands)*		*Percent*	*U.S. dollars per kilogram*		*Percent*
Sugar and related products	193	801	316	--	--	--	--	--	--
Confectionery products, except chewing gum	29	403	1,267	18	136	649	1.64	2.97	81
Maple syrup	28	159	460	12	23	98	2.49	6.99	181
Glucose and glucose syrup	15	67	339	69	169	146	0.22	0.40	79
Chewing gum	30	61	103	17	25	53	1.80	2.41	34
Other	89	111	24	--	--	--	--	--	--
Cocoa and cocoa products	148	992	572	78	284	263	1.89	3.49	84
Chocolate or cocoa preparations in blocks, slabs, or bars of 2 kilograms or more, or in liquid, paste, powder, granular, or other bulk form in containers or immediate packaging of a content exceeding 2 kilograms	56	394	605	37	165	339	1.49	2.40	60
Chocolate or cocoa preparations, in bars, blocks, or slabs not over 2 kilograms, filled	28	131	371	11	22	96	2.45	5.90	141
Chocolate or cocoa preparations, in bars, blocks, or slabs not over 2 kilograms, not filled	4	111	2,728	1	17	1,411	3.53	6.60	87
Chocolate or cocoa preparations, not elsewhere specified	52	322	518	23	71	205	2.23	4.51	103
Other	8	33	327	--	--	--	--	--	--

Appendix table 2. (Continued)

	Value			Volume			Unit Value		
	1991 -93	2011 -13	Change	1991 -93	2011 -13	Change	1991 -93	2011 -13	Change
	U.S. dollars (millions)		*Percent*	*Metric tons (thousands)*		*Percent*	*U.S. dollars per kilogram*		*Percent*
Coffee and coffee products	33	405	1,126	6	38	567	5.79	10.58	83
Coffee, roasted, not decaffeinated, in retail containers weighing 2 kilograms or less	3	290	8,305	1	26	3,519	4.84	11.27	133
Coffee, roasted, not decaffeinated, other	1	60	10,914	*	7	5,573	4.64	9.01	94
Other	29	55	90	--	--	--	--	--	--
Tea and mate, including herbal tea	24	107	357	37	58	57	0.67	1.85	177
Preparations of tea or mate containing over 10 percent by dry weight of sugar	--	72	--	--	56	--	--	1.29	--
Other	--	36	--	--	--	--	--		--
Spices and herbs	21	74	254	60	79	31	0.35	0.93	170
Mustard seeds	15	52	239	55	65	18	0.28	0.80	187
Other	5	22	295	--	--	--	--		--
Tobacco, unmanufactured	27	88	226	9	19	110	3.01	4.68	55
Beverages, excluding fruit juices	196	374	92	--	--	--	--	--	--
Beer made from malt[6]	148	185	25	262	252	-4	0.57	0.73	30
Preparations for beverages	5	74	1,354	4	44	959	1.24	1.70	37
Other	43	115	169	--	--	--	--	--	--
Oilseeds and products	50	270	442	73	206	182	0.68	1.31	92
Rapeseed oil	151	1,775	1,079	297	1,403	372	0.50	1.27	151

	Value			Volume			Unit Value		
	1991 -93	2011 -13	Change	1991 -93	2011 -13	Change	1991 -93	2011 -13	Change
	U.S. dollars (millions)		*Percent*	*Metric tons (thousands)*		*Percent*	*U.S. dollars per kilogram*		*Percent*
Rape or colza seed oilcake	67	866	1,195	520	2,782	435	0.21	0.31	51
Rapeseed	13	291	2,167	55	553	908	0.25	0.53	107
Soybeans	21	220	968	96	410	329	0.22	0.54	149
Soybean oil	1	91	9,662	2	73	3,808	0.50	1.24	150
Flaxseed	24	120	399	130	177	36	0.19	0.68	261
Other	42	342	718	--	--	--	--	--	--
Seeds, field and garden	50	270	442	73	206	182	0.68	1.31	92
Corn seed	9	77	775	7	19	158	1.22	4.12	239
Other	41	192	370	--	--	--	--	--	--
Nursery stock, bulbs, etc.	85	245	189	--	--	--	--	--	--
Other horticultural products	82	673	724	--	--	--	--	--	--
Soups, broths, and preparations, not dried, not based on fish or seafood	5	118	2,294	4	99	2,666	1.68	1.19	-29
Yeasts	16	81	425	18	53	185	0.84	1.55	84
Other	61	474	674	--	--	--	--	--	--
Other	37	139	280	--	--	--	--	--	--

[*] Less than $500,000 in value and 500 kilograms in volume.

[1] Volume is measured in thousands of head, and unit value is measured in dollars per head.

[2] Volume is measured in thousands of furskins, and unit value is measured in dollars per furskin.

[3] Volume is measured in thousands of pieces, and unit value is measured in dollars per piece.

[4] Excludes stuffed pasta and canned pasta.

[5] Excludes seed potatoes.

[6] Volume is measured in millions of liters, and unit value is measured in dollars per liter.

Source: Prepared by USDA Economic Research Service, using data from U.S. Department of Commerce, Bureau of the Census, *Foreign Trade Statistics*, as presented by USDA/FAS (2014a).

Appendix table 3. Selected U.S. agricultural exports to Mexico, 1991-93 versus 2011-13

	Value			Volume			Unit Value		Change
	Average annual		Change	Average annual		Change	For period		
	1991-93	2011-13		1991-93	2011-13		1991-93	2011-13	
	U.S. dollars (millions)		*Percent*	*Metric tons (thousands)*		*Percent*	*U.S. dollars per kilogram*		*Percent*
Total	3,475	18,455	431	--	--	--	--	--	--
Animals and animal products	1,183	5,306	348	--	--	--	--	--	--
Pork	68	891	1,210	32	426	1,232	2.15	2.09	-3
Pork variety meats	46	198	331	62	147	138	0.73	1.34	83
Beef and veal	171	692	305	58	133	129	2.97	5.21	76
Beef variety meats	48	219	356	41	89	118	1.18	2.45	108
Nonfat dry milk	55	635	1,055	33	188	470	1.64	3.38	106
Chickens, fresh or frozen	68	583	758	74	550	644	0.92	1.06	15
Tallow, inedible	41	292	613	113	275	143	0.36	1.06	192
Turkeys, fresh or frozen	66	337	411	46	172	274	1.42	1.96	38
Cheese	14	275	1,801	5	65	1,097	2.62	4.21	61
Whey, fluid or dried	12	133	1,001	--	--	--	--	--	--
Tallow, edible	33	68	110	89	64	-28	0.37	1.07	192

	Value			Volume			Unit Value		Change
	Average annual		Change	Average annual		Change	For period		
	1991-93	2011-13		1991-93	2011-13		1991-93	2011-13	
	U.S. dollars (millions)		*Percent*	*Metric tons (thousands)*		*Percent*	*U.S. dollars per kilogram*		*Percent*
Bovine hides, whole[1]	110	66	-40	2,415	1,244	-48	45.43	52.75	16
Live horses[2]	2	61	3,512	2	129	6,578	876.00	473.74	-46
Cattle and calves[2]	115	26	-77	179	17	-90	680.57	1,522.64	124
Other	334	828	148	--	--	--	--	--	--
Grains and feeds	897	5,406	503	6,507	16,307	151	0.14	0.33	141
Corn	104	2,314	2,126	913	7,870	762	0.12	0.29	153
Brewing or distilling dregs and waste	2	414	23,451	15	1,521	10,113	0.11	0.27	143
Cracked corn	13	56	344	69	155	125	0.22	0.36	68
Wheat, unmilled	78	1,016	1,202	563	3,238	475	0.14	0.31	127
Sorghum	428	427	0	3,949	1,535	-61	0.11	0.28	158
Rice	42	375	793	175	874	400	0.25	0.43	74
Malt, not roasted	13	130	923	59	226	286	0.28	0.57	104
Other bread, pastry, cake, biscuits, and bakery, wares, excluding pizza and quiche	18	96	439	13	17	29	1.32	5.52	317
Preparations used in animal feeding, except pet food and bird seed	37	78	109	179	61	-66	0.21	1.27	512

Appendix table 3. (Continued)

	Value			Volume			Unit Value		
	Average annual		Change	Average annual		Change	For period		Change
	1991-93	2011-13		1991-93	2011-13		1991-93	2011-13	
	U.S. dollars (millions)		*Percent*	*Metric tons (thousands)*		*Percent*	*U.S. dollars per kilogram*		*Percent*
Mixes and doughs	--	72	--	--	48	--	--	1.50	--
Other	162	429	164	--	--	--	--	--	--
Fruits and preparations, excluding juice	81	645	694	143	527	269	0.57	1.22	114
Apples, fresh	34	272	700	68	237	249	0.52	1.15	122
Pears, fresh	17	81	382	33	80	142	0.51	1.01	99
Grapes, fresh	5	77	1,509	5.13	48	842	0.93	1.59	71
Other	26	216	738	--	--	--	--	--	--
Nuts and preparations	33	246	636	22	70	216	1.51	3.53	133
Pecans	13	63	393	6	10	62	2	6.18	204
Other	21	183	786	--	--	--	--	--	--
Vegetables and preparations	96	603	530	--	--	--	--	--	--
Dry common beans	15	112	634	26	133	408	0.58	0.84	44
Potatoes, frozen	7	91	1,284	10	91	829	0.69	1.00	44
Sauces and preparations, not elsewhere specified	5	55	1,005	2	29	1,120	2.13	1.93	-9

	Value			Volume			Unit Value		Change
	Average annual		Change	Average annual		Change	For period		
	1991-93	2011-13		1991-93	2011-13		1991-93	2011-13	
	U.S. dollars (millions)		*Percent*	*Metric tons (thousands)*		*Percent*	*U.S. dollars per kilogram*		*Percent*
Other	69	345	401	--	--	--	--	--	--
Oilseeds and products	633	3,091	389	2,489	5,286	112	0.25	0.58	130
Soybeans	400	1,686	321	718	3,066	327	0.23	0.55	136
Soybean meal	68	634	832	313	1,345	330	0.23	0.47	107
Soybean oil	13	205	1,474	27	169	525	0.47	1.21	156
Animal or vegetable fats and oils and their fractions, not elsewhere specified	3	75	2,152	27	87	223	0.47	0.86	81
Other	148	492	232	--	--	--	--	--	--
Tobacco, unmanufactured	*	90	42,477	*	16	30,085	3.75	5.56	48
Cotton, excluding linters	118	532	350	87	221	154	1.42	2.41	69
Essential oils	21	106	395	2	8	292	10.46	13.40	28
Mixtures of odoriferous substances for use in food and beverage industry	2	74	2,998	*	5	1,831	8.46	13.56	60
Other	19	33	71	--	--	--	--	--	--
Seeds, field and garden	108	245	127	181	117	-35	0.76	2.10	176
Sugar and tropical products	154	1,255	717	--	--	--	--	--	--
Fructose syrup, containing more than 50 percent by weight of fructose, NESOI	5	445	8,627	17	1,136	6,781	0.31	0.39	24

Appendix table 3. (Continued)

	Value			Volume			Unit Value		Change
	Average annual		Change	Average annual		Change	For period		
	1991-93	2011-13		1991-93	2011-13		1991-93	2011-13	
	U.S. dollars (millions)		*Percent*	*Metric tons (thousands)*		*Percent*	*U.S. dollars per kilogram*		*Percent*
Chocolate and preparations	47	230	390	16	63	294	2.92	3.62	24
Glucose or glucose syrup	5	187	3,388	18	424	2,237	0.37	0.44	19
Sugar, cane or beet	44	120	170	116	148	28	0.36	0.81	126
Other	52	274	428	--	--	--	--	--	--
Other horticulutural products	60	631	954	--	--	--	--	--	--
Soups, broths, and preparations thereof, dried	18	176	868	9	66	592	1.91	2.69	41
Other	42	454	991	--	--	--	--	--	--
Nursery and greenhouse products	15	55	268	--	--	--	--	--	--
Beverages, excluding juices	51	193	277	--	--	--	--	--	--
Beer from malt[3]	12	108	765	22	132	490	0.55	0.81	48
Other	39	86	120	--	--	--	--	--	--
Other	25	51	100	--	--	--	--	--	--

Unit value is calculated as the average of the annual unit values for the 3 years in the period specified.

*Less than $500,000 in average value and less than 500 metric tons in average volume.

[1]Volume is measured in thousands of pieces, and unit value is measured in dollars per piece.

[2]Volume is measured in thousands of head, and unit value is measured in dollars per head.

[3] Volume is measured in millions of liters, and unit value is measured in dollars per liter.

Source: USDA, Economic Research Service, using U.S. Department of Commerce, Census Bureau, *Foreign Trade Statistics*, as cited by USDA/FAS (2014a).

Appendix table 4. Selected U.S. agricultural imports to Mexico, 1991-93 versus 2011-13

	Value			**Volume**			**Unit Value**		**Change**
	Average annual		**Change**	**Average annual**		**Change**	**For period**		
	1991-93	**2011-13**		**1991-93**	**2011-13**		**1991-93**	**2011-13**	
	U.S. dollars (millions)		*Percent*	*Metric tons (thousands)*		*Percent*	*U.S. dollars per kilogram*		*Percent*
Total	2,542	16,635	554	--	--	--	--	--	--
Animals and animal products	408	1,370	236	--	--	--	--	--	--
Cattle and calves[1]	377	614	63	1,104	1,293	17	342.67	474.79	39
Beef and veal	2	460	22,876	1	81	12,274	3.51	5.71	63
Milk and cream, fresh or dried	--	55	--	--	--	--	--	--	--
Parings and similar waste of raw hides or skins, or glue stock not elsewhere specified or included	1	51	6,155	*	11	3,470	2.65	4.65	75
Other	28	189	572	--	--	--	--	--	--

Appendix table 4. (Continued)

	Value			Volume			Unit Value		
	Average annual		Change	Average annual		Change	For period		Change
	1991 -93	2011 -13		1991 -93	2011 -13		1991 -93	2011 -13	
	U.S. dollars (millions)		*Percent*	*Metric tons (thousands)*		*Percent*	*U.S. dollars per kilogram*		*Percent*
Grains and feeds	51	949	1,756						
Biscuits and wafers[2]	16	485	2,961	11	212	1,857	1.46	2.28	57
Prepared foods obtained from swelling or roasting of cereal flakes or products, with or without sugar	4	145	3,895	2	44	1,673	1.47	3.33	127
Corn chips and savory snacks	11	93	746	7	35	413	1.63	2.67	64
Pastry, not elsewhere specified or indicated	13	74	491	8	30	259	1.52	2.51	65
Pasta and noodles	5	52	992	6	57	840	0.78	0.91	16
Other	3	100	2,834	--	--	--	--	--	--
Fruits and preparations	322	3,322	932	586	2,825	382	0.45	1.18	159
Avocados, fresh or dried	1	841	82,902	1	420	74,886	1.85	2.00	9
Avocados, processed	12	137	1,015	6	51	788	2.16	2.71	26
Strawberries, fresh	15	300	1,902	12	140	1,063	1.28	2.15	69
Strawberries, frozen	18	111	505	23	77	237	0.80	1.43	80

	Value			Volume			Unit Value		
	Average annual		Change	Average annual		Change	For period		Change
	1991-93	2011-13		1991-93	2011-13		1991-93	2011-13	
	U.S. dollars (millions)		*Percent*	*Metric tons (thousands)*		*Percent*	*U.S. dollars per kilogram*		*Percent*
Grapes, fresh	59	326	452	40	136	241	1.47	2.39	63
Watermelons, fresh	18	226	1,157	89	459	415	0.20	0.49	149
Limes, fresh or dried	20	198	875	87	401	364	0.23	0.49	110
Mangoes, fresh[3]	63	194	208	80	253	216	0.79	0.77	-2
Raspberries, fresh	*	193	1,232,447	*	25	471,622	2.93	7.58	159
Blackberries, mulberries, and loganberries, fresh	*	174	317,529	*	51	127,018	1.45	3.41	135
Bananas, fresh	84	89	6	307	209	-32	0.27	0.42	55
Grapefruit, prepared or preserved	3	63	2,108	3	36	1,266	1.10	1.77	62
Papayas, fresh	4	57	1,325	7	107	1,338	0.53	0.54	2
Other	24	412	1,583	--	--	--	--	--	--
Fruit juices[4]	40	216	443	147	484	228	0.29	0.45	53
Orange juice[4]	22	150	577	97	367	279	0.23	0.41	74
Other	18	67	276	--	--	--	--	--	--
Nuts and preparations	55	324	487	17	76	335	3.35	4.26	27
Pecans	53	269	403	14	45	222	4.02	5.91	47

Appendix table 4. (Continued)

	Value			Volume			Unit Value		
	Average annual		Change	Average annual		Change	For period		Change
	1991-93	2011-13		1991-93	2011-13		1991-93	2011-13	
	U.S. dollars (millions)		*Percent*	*Metric tons (thousands)*		*Percent*	*U.S. dollars per kilogram*		*Percent*
Other	2	55	2,954	--	--	--	--	--	--
Vegetables and preparations	923	5,049	447	--	--	--	--	--	--
Tomatoes, fresh	229	1,674	631	312	1,363	337	0.73	1.23	68
Peppers, fresh	120	755	530	124	726	485	0.97	1.04	8
Cucumbers, fresh	73	345	373	179	527	195	0.41	0.65	60
Squash, fresh	60	259	332	83	285	244	0.72	0.91	26
Asparagus, fresh	29	257	785	21	96	357	1.39	2.67	92
Onions, fresh	92	226	146	178	258	45	0.52	0.88	68
Broccoli, frozen	89	220	146	133	198	49	0.67	1.11	65
Lettuce, fresh	4	146	3,882	8	141	1,564	0.44	1.03	135
Cauliflower and broccoli, fresh	4	133	3,446	13	149	1,025	0.28	0.89	219
Sauces and preparations, not elsewhere specified	--	81	--	--	56	--	--	1.45	--
Potato granules	--	65	--	--	17	--	--	3.86	--
Fresh beans, other than vigna, lima, or lentils	12	55	365	10	42	307	1.13	1.29	14

	Value			Volume			Unit Value		
	Average annual		Change	Average annual		Change	For period		Change
	1991-93	2011-13		1991-93	2011-13		1991-93	2011-13	
	U.S. dollars (millions)		*Percent*	*Metric tons (thousands)*		*Percent*	*U.S. dollars per kilogram*		*Percent*
Eggplant, fresh	12	50	303	18	49	172	0.69	1.02	48
Other	199	782	293	--	--	--	--	--	--
Sugar and related products	35	1,596	4,399	--	--	--	--	--	--
Sugar, cane or beet	1	1,057	89,104	3	1,514	57,404	0.82	0.70	-15
Confectionery products	23	445	1,869	15	209	1,332	1.54	2.13	38
Other	12	94	701	--	--	--	--	--	--
Cocoa and cocoa products	20	516	2,503	14	215	1,480	1.69	2.40	42
Coffee and coffee products	279	554	99	182	111	-39	1.53	4.99	225
Coffee, arabica, not roasted, not decaffeinated	25	325	1,194	17	74	332	1.48	4.42	199
Instant coffee, not flavored, not decaffeinated, packaged for retail sale	1	94	13,871	*	11	4,648	4.85	8.63	78
Coffee, arabica, not roasted, decaffeinated	30	55	83	10	12	4,648	3.00	4.67	56
Other	223	79	-64	--	--	--	--	--	--
Spices and herbs	41	72	76	28	43	54	1.45	1.65	14
Drugs, crude natural	2	59	2,934	4	21	470	0.52	2.76	432

Appendix table 4. (Continued)

	Value			Volume			Unit Value		
	Average annual		Change	Average annual		Change	For period		Change
	1991-93	2011-13		1991-93	2011-13		1991-93	2011-13	
	U.S. dollars (millions)		*Percent*	*Metric tons (thousands)*		*Percent*	*U.S. dollars per kilogram*		*Percent*
Essential oils	8	51	500	--	--	--	--	--	--
Beverages, excluding fruit juices	170	2,118	1,146	--	--	--	--	--	--
Beer[4]	145	1,804	1,144	179	1,770	889	0.82	1.02	24
Carbonated soft drinks[4]	15	204	1,261	19	298	1,468	0.80	0.69	-15
Other nonalcoholic beverages[4]	6	73	1,095	8	96	1,090	0.75	0.76	0
Other	4	37	837	--	--	--	--	--	--
Oilseeds and oilseed products	38	146	285	32	78	148	1.14	1.86	63
Other horticultural products	52	173	229	--	--	--	--	--	--
Yeasts	10	70	584	7	25	270	1.52	2.82	85
Other	42	103	143	--	--	--	--	--	--
Other	97	122	25	--	--	--	--	--	--

* = Imports average less than $500,000 in value and/or less than 500 metric tons in volume.

[1]Volume is measured in thousands of head, and unit value is measured in dollars per head.

[2]Includes sweet biscuits, waffles, wafers, pastries, cake, and bread, among other products.

[3]Data for 1991-92 also include guavas and mangosteens.

[4]Volume is measured in millions of liters, and unit value is measured in dollars per liter.

Source: USDA, Economic Research Service, using U.S. Department of Commerce, Census Bureau, *Foreign Trade Statistics*, as cited by USDA/FAS (2014a).

Appendix table 5. U.S., Canadian, and Mexican foreign direct investment position in the NAFTA region's food industry on a historical-cost basis

	Food and kindred products				
Origin/destination	**1994**	**1995**	**1996**	**1997**	**1998**
	U.S. million dollars				
U.S. direct investment in Canada	4,021	4,498	4,265	4,649	4,985
U.S. direct investment in Mexico	2,660	2,929	3,579	4,484	4,723
Canadian direct investment in the U.S.	5,877	7,199	7,764	10,087	6,684
Mexican direct investment in the U.S.	(S)	(S)	(S)	306	1,092

	Food industry														
Origin/destination	**1999**	**2000**	**2001**	**2002**	**2003**	**2004**	**2005**	**2006**	**2007**	**2008**	**2009**	**2010**	**2011**	**2012**	**2013**
U.S. direct investment in Canada	3,693	3,431	3,421	4,153	3,964	2,821	2,718	2,998	4,393	4,458	5,090	6,079	7,655	8,599	10,143
U.S. direct investment in Mexico	1,281	1,427	1,250	2,159	2,134	2,203	2,790	2,610	2,835	2,497	2,971	3,271	3,728	3,894	3,983
Canadian direct investment in the U.S.	1,088	1,405	984	983	922	1,175	2,109	1,235	1,200	995	945	1,220	1,655	1,957	1,846
Mexican direct investment in the U.S.	1,060	1,058	1,102	(S)	(S)	(S)	(S)	(S)	(S)	1,303	(S)	(S)	1,947	2,034	2,187

Note: Kindred products refers primarily to beverages. NAFTA = North American Free Trade Agreement.

(S) = Suppressed in order to avoid disclosure of data of individual companies

Source: USDA, Economic Research Service, using U.S. Department of Commerce, Bureau of Economic Analysis (2014a).

REFERENCES

Agriculture and Agri-Food Canada. (2013). "Canada's Agri-Food and Seafood Trade With the World." Webpage. March 8. http://www.ats-sea.agr.gc.ca/stats/da-do-eng.htm (accessed January 6, 2015).

Arnold, Bruce. (2003). *The Effects of NAFTA on U.S.-Mexican Trade and GDP*. Congressional Budget Office. May. www.cbo.gov.

Avendaño Ruiz, Belem Dolores, Ana Isabel Acosta Martínez, & Rita Schwentesius. (2014). "La Integración de los Mercados Hortícolas de México y los Estados Unidos." Paper presented at the Congress of the Latin American Studies Association, Chicago, Illinois, May 21-24.

Balassa, Bela. (1961). *The Theory of Economic Integration*. Homewood, Illinois: R.D. Irwin.

Branson, Adam. (2011). *Mexico Lifts Ban on Poultry from Polk County Missouri*. U.S. Department of Agriculture, Foreign Agricultural Service, Global Agricultural Information Network Report No. MX1090, December 5. http://gain.fas.usda.gov/Recent%20GAIN%20Publications/Mexico%20 Lifts%20Ban%20on%20Poultry%20from%20Polk%20County%20Missouri_Mexico_ Mexico_12-5-2011.pdf (accessed March 31, 2014).

Branson, Adam, & Gabriel Hernandez. (2014). *Mexican Market Opened to U.S. Beef and Beef By-Products of All Ages*. U.S. Department of Agriculture, Foreign Agricultural Service, Global Agricultural Information Network Report No. MX4036, April 29. http://gain.fas.usda. gov/Recent%20GAIN%20Publications/Mexican%20Market%20Opened% 20to%20U.S.%20Beef%20and%20Beef%20By-Products%20of%20All% 20Ages_Mexico_Mexico_4-29-2014.pdf (accessed July 14, 2014).

Canada Border Services Agency. (2014). *Measures in Force: Goods subject to anti-dumping or countervailing duties*. September 11. http://www.cbsa-asfc.gc.ca/sima-lmsi/mif-mev-eng.html (accessed October 9, 2014).

Canada Dairy Information Centre. (2013). "Per capita consumption of dairy products." September 30. http://www.dairyinfo.gc.ca/pdf/dpconsumption_ e.pdf (accessed March 18, 2014).

Canadian Cattlemen's Association. (2009). "Mandatory Country-of-Origin Labeling: Impact on Beef Industry." www.cattle.ca/impact-on-beef-cattle-industry (accessed March 4, 2011).

Canadian Food Inspection Agency. (2014). "BSE Enhanced Surveillance Program." Webpage. March 28. www.inspection.gc.ca/english/anima/ disemala/bseesb/bseesbe.shtml (accessed March 31, 2014).

Carter, Colin A. & Loyns, R. M. A. (1996). *The Economics of Single Desk Selling of Western Canadian Grain*. March. http://rolfpennerforcwb. files.wordpress.com/2008/09/carter-loyns- singledeskselling.pdf (accessed May 13, 2014).

Cook, Roberta, & Linda, Calvin. (2005). *Greenhouse Tomatoes Change the Dynamics of the North American Fresh Tomato Industry*. U.S. Department of Agriculture, Economic Research Service, Economic Research Report No. 2, April. www.ers.usda.gov/publications/err2/ (accessed January 25, 2011).

Crawford, Terry & John, Link (team leaders). (1997). *NAFTA: International Agriculture and Trade*. U.S. Department of Agriculture, Economic Research Service, Outlook Report No. WRS-97-2, September 3. www.ers.usda.gov/briefing/nafta/ mandated.htm (accessed February 20, 2007).

Dessureault, Darlene. (2013). *Food Safety Modernization Act Outreach Fall 2013 Session*. U.S. Department of Agriculture, Foreign Agricultural Service, Global Agricultural Information Network Report No. CA 13049, October 2. http://gain.fas.usda.gov/Recent%20GAIN%20 Publications/ Food%20Safety%20Modernization%20Act%20Outreach%20Fall%20201 3%20 Session_Ottawa_Canada_10-02-2013.pdf (accessed May 12, 2014).

Executive Office of the President of the United States. (2013). Letter from Ambassador Ron Kirk to the Honorable Irving Williamson, Chairman of the USITC. March 11. http://www.usitc.gov/research_and_analysis/ ongoing/documents/NAFTA_rules_or_origin_request.pdf (accessed June 4, 2014).

Flores, Dulce, Mark, Ford & Carlos, A. Gonzales. (2010). *Mexico Sugar Semi-Annual*. U.S. Department of Agriculture, Foreign Agricultural Service, Global Agricultural Information Network No. MX0023, April 15. http:// gain.fas.usda.gov/Recent%20GAIN%20Publications/ SUGAR%20 SEMI-ANNUAL_Mexico_Mexico_11-6-2009.pdf (accessed May 7, 2014).

Flores, Dulce, & Pete Olson. (2013a). *Mexico Avocado Annual: Overall Production Forecast Up Slightly But Weather In Michoacán May Reduce Exports*. U.S. Department of Agriculture, Foreign Agricultural Service, Global Agricultural Information Network No. MX3086, December 19. http://gain.fas.usda.gov/Recent%20GAIN%20Publications/Avocado%20 Annual_Mexico%20City_Mexico_12-19-2013.pdf (accessed June 17, 2014).

____. (2013b). *Mexico Tomato Annual: Tomato Suspension Agreement Key to Production and Trade Forecasts*. U.S. Department of Agriculture, Foreign

Agricultural Service, Global Agricultural Information Network No. MX3045, May 31. http://gain.fas.usda.gov/Recent% 20GAIN% 20Publications/Tomato%20Annual_Mexico%20City_Mexico_5-31-2013.pdf (accessed July 17, 2014).

Fresh Produce Alliance. (2014). "Canada Loses Preferred Access to the US Perishable Agricultural Commodities Act." *PerishableNews.com*, October 6. http://www.perishablenews.com/index. php?article=0039764 (accessed October 20, 2014).

Fruit and Vegetable Dispute Resolution Corporation (DRC). (2014a). "Dispute Resolution." Webpage. http://www.fvdrc.com/en/home/mediation/dispute-resolution-system.aspx (accessed May 12, 2014).

____. (2014b). "What We Do." Webpage. http://www.fvdrc.com/en/home/about/what-we-do.aspx (accessed May 12, 2014).

____. (2007). "DRC Mexico Closes Operations – Services to be Continued from Ottawa Headquarters." Press release, August 30. www.fvdrc.com/adx/aspx/adxGetMedia.aspx?DocID=484,70,8,1,Documents&MediaID=6721&Filename=Aug_30_07_Press_Release_DRC_Mex_ Closes_eng.pdf (accessed December 22, 2010).

Ghazalian, Pascal L., Bruno, Larue & Jean-Philippe, Gervais. (2011). "Accessing the Implications of Regional Preferential Market Access for Meat Commodities." *Agribusiness*, Vol. *27*, No. 3, 292-310.

Global Trade Information Services. (2014). *Global Trade Atlas.* Columbia, South Carolina. Gómez, Miguel I., Maleeha Rizwan, and Katie Ricketts. 2012. *Origin, Creation, and Evolution of the Fruit & Vegetable Dispute Resolution Corporation.* Final report prepared for the U.S. Department of Agriculture, Agricultural Marketing Service, under Cooperative Agreement #12-25-A-5124, January. http://www.fvdrc.com/media/14918/drc_history_project_final_report. pdf (accessed May 12, 2014).

Goodloe, Carol. (2004). "The Canadian Wheat Board: Government Guarantees and Hidden Subsidies?" *The Estey Centre Journal of International Law and Trade Policy*, *5*(2), 102-22. www.esteycentre.ca/journal/

Government of Canada. (2013). *Opening New Markets in Europe: Creating Jobs and Opportunities for Canadians. Technical Summary of Final Negotiated Outcomes: Canada-European Union Comprehensive Economic and Trade Agreement: Agreement-in-Principle*. October. http://www.actionplan.gc.ca/sites/default/files/pdfs/ceta-technicalsummary.pdf (accessed March 18, 2014).

Green, Tina, Lynne Hansen, Ling Lee, Hector Fanghanel, & Steven Zahniser. (2006). "North American Approaches to Regulatory Coordination." In *Achieving NAFTA Plus*, edited by K. Huff, K. Meilke, R. Knutson, R. Ochoa, and J. Rude, 9-47. Texas A&M University, University of Guelph, and Inter-American Institute for Cooperation on Agriculture-Mexico. http://naamic. tamu.edu/sanantonio/green.pdf (accessed November 21, 2008).

Hahn, William, Mildred Haley, Dale Leuck, James Miller, Janet Perry, Fawzi Taha, & Steven Zahniser. (2005). *Market Integration of the North American Animal Products Complex*. U.S. Department of Agriculture, Economic Research Service, Outlook Report No. LDP-M-131-01, May. http://www.ers.usda.gov/publications/ldpm-livestock,-dairy,-and-poultry-outlook/ldpm13101.aspx (accessed July 17, 2014).

Haley, Stephen. (2014a). "Sugar and Sweetener Yearbook Tables: Table 24b: U.S. Sugar: Supply and Use (including Puerto Rico), fiscal years, metric tons." U.S. Department of Agriculture, Economic Research Service, April 10. www.ers.usda.gov/Briefing/Sugar/data.htm#yearbook (accessed May 8, 2014).

____. (2014b). "Sugar and Sweetener Yearbook Tables: Table 34a: U.S. Exports of High Fructose Corn Syrup to Mexico," U.S. Department of Agriculture, Economic Research Service, January 15. http://www.ers.usda.gov/data-products/sugar-and-sweeteners-yearbook-tables.aspx (accessed February 7, 2014).

____. (2014c). *Sugar and Sweeteners Outlook*. U.S. Department of Agriculture, Economic Research Service, Outlook Report No. SSS-M-305. January 16. http://usda.mannlib.cornell.edu/usda/ers/ SSS//2010s/ 2014/SSS-01-16-2014.pdf (accessed May 6, 2014).

____. (2013). "Sugar and Sweetener Yearbook Tables: Table 30: U.S. High Fructose Corn Syrup (HFCS) Supply and Use." U.S. Department of Agriculture, Economic Research Service, March 10. http://www.ers. usda.gov/data-products/sugar-and-sweeteners-yearbook-tables.aspx# 25480 (accessed May 8, 2014)

Hebbar, Prakash K. (2014). "Citrus Greening (HLB) Quarantine and Control." Presentation deliv- ered at the 2014 Agricultural Outlook Forum, U.S. Department of Agriculture, Arlington, VA, February 21. http://www. usda.gov/oce/forum/friday.htm#friday10 (accessed July 17, 2014).

Hernandez, Gabriel. (2013). *Mexico Livestock and Products Annual*. U.S. Department of Agriculture, Foreign Agricultural Service, Global Agricultural Information Network Report No. MX3062, August 16.

http://gain.fas.usda.gov/Recent%20GAIN%20Publications/Livestock%20 and%20 Products%20Annual_Mexico%20City_Mexico_8-16-2013.pdf (accessed September 16, 2014).

Hernandez, Gabriel & Adam Branson. (2013). *Mexico Poultry and Products Annual.* U.S. Department of Agriculture, Foreign Agricultural Service, Global Agricultural Information Network Report No. MX3066, August 30. http://gain.fas.usda.gov/Recent%20GAIN%20Publications/Poultry%20and%20Products%20Annual_Mexico%20City_Mexico_8-30-2013.pdf (accessed March 31, 2014).

____. (2011). *Mexico Dairy and Products Annual.* U.S. Department of Agriculture, Foreign Agricultural Service, Global Agricultural Information Network Report No. MX1083, November 14. http://gain.fas.usda.gov/Recent%20GAIN%20Publications/Dairy%20and%20Products%20Annual_Mexico%20City_Mexico_11-14-2011.pdf (accessed March 31, 2014).

Hernandez, Gabriel, Luis Chavez, & Adam Branson. (2014). *Livestock and Products Semi-annual.* U.S. Department of Agriculture, Foreign Agricultural Service, Global Agricultural Information Network Report No. MX4015, March 1. http://gain.fas.usda.gov/Recent%20GAIN%20Publications/Livestock%20and%20Products%20Semi-annual_Mexico%20City_Mexico_3-2-2014.pdf (accessed September 16, 2014).

Hernandez, Gabriel, Luis Chavez & Pete Olson. (2014). *Poultry and Products Annual.* U.S. Department of Agriculture, Foreign Agricultural Service, Global Agricultural Information Network Report No. MX4061, August 18. http://gain.fas.usda.gov/Recent%20GAIN%20Publications/Poultry%20and%20Products%20Annual_Mexico%20City_Mexico_8-18-2014.pdf (accessed September 16, 2014).

Hernandez, Gabriel, Vanessa Salcido & Adam Branson. (2013). *Mexico Dairy and Products Annual.* U.S. Department of Agriculture, Foreign Agricultural Service, Global Agricultural Information Network Report No. MX3076, October 28. http://gain.fas.usda.gov/Recent %20GAIN%20Publications/Dairy%20and%20Products%20Annual_Mexico%20City_Mexico_10-28-2013.pdf (accessed March 31, 2014).

Hertz, Tom. (2013). "Farm Labor: Background." Webpage. U.S. Department of Agriculture, Economic Research Service. February 14. http://www.ers.usda.gov/topics/farm-economy/farm-labor/background.aspx#legalstatus (accessed October 10, 2014).

Jabara, Cathy L. & Brendan Lynch. (2006). "Exports and New Varieties: An Analysis of U.S.- Mexico Agricultural Trade." U.S. International Trade

Commission, Office of Industries, Working Paper No. ID-16, September. www.usitc.gov/publications/332/working_papers/WorkingPaperID16mexcj.pdf (accessed December 28, 2010).

James, Cheryl & Mark, Davidson. (2014). "Zoning for Foreign Animal Disease: Presentation to RCC Stakeholder Dialogue Session." February 7. http://www.trade.gov/rcc/rcc-webinar-presentations-january2014.asp (accessed April 1, 2014).

Jayasinghe, Sampath, & Rakhal Sarker. (2008). "Effects of Regional Trade Agreements on Trade in Agrifood Products: Evidence from Gravity Modeling Using Disaggregated Data." *Review of Agricultural Economics*, Vol. *30*, No. 1, 61-81.

Juarez, Benjamin. (2014). *Mexico Grain and Feed Annual 2014*. U.S. Department of Agriculture, Foreign Agriculture Service, Global Agriculture Information Network Report No. MX4020, March 14. http://gain.fas.usda.gov/Recent%20GAIN%20Publications/Grain%20and%20Feed%20Annual_Mexico%20City_Mexico_3-14-2014.pdf (accessed May 13, 2014).

Lambert, David & Shahera McKoy. (2009). "Trade Creation and Diversion Effects of Preferential Trade Associations on Agricultural and Food Trade." *Journal of Agricultural Economics*, Vol. *60*, No. 1, 17-39.

Linden, Tim. (2014). "USDA Revokes Preferred PACA Treatment for Canadian Shippers." *The Produce News*, October 3. http://producenews.com/news-dep-menu/test-featured/14231-usda- revokes-preferred-paca-treatment-for-canadian-shippers(accessed October 20, 2014).

Martin, Phil. (2013). "Immigration Reform 2013: Implications for California Agriculture," *ARE Update*, Vol. *16*, No. 5, May/June, University of California, Giannini Foundation of Agricultural Economics, 5-8. http://giannini.ucop.edu/media/are-update/files/articles/V16N5_2.pdf (accessed July 14, 2014).

Meilke, Karl, James Rude, & Steven Zahniser. (2008). "Is 'NAFTA Plus' an Option in the North American Agrifood Sector." *The World Economy*, Vol. *31*, Issue 7 (July), 925-946.

México, Secretaría de Agricultura, Ganadería, Desarrollo Rural, Pesca, y Alimentación (SAGARPA). (2014a). "Decreto por el que se aprueba el Programa Nacional de la Agroindustria de la Caña de Azúcar 2014-2018." *Diario Oficial de la Federación*, May 2. http://dof.gob.mx/ nota_detalle.php?codigo=5343243&fecha=02/05/2014 (accessed May 9, 2014).

___. (2014b). "Programa Nacional de la Agroindustria de la Caña de Azúcar." *Diario Oficial dela Federación*, May 2. http://dof.gob.mx/nota_detalle.php?codigo=5343244&fecha=02/05/2014 (accessed May 9, 2014).

México, Secretaría de Agricultura, Ganadería, Desarrollo Rural, Pesca, y Alimentación, Servicio de Información Agroalimentaria y Pesquera (SAGARPA/SIAP). (2014a). "Cierre de la Producción Agrícola por Cultivo." Interactive database. www.siap.gob.mx/index.php?option=com_wrapper&view=wrapper&Itemid=350 (accessed June 16, 2014).

_______. (2014b). *Resumen Nacional Pecuario*. Interactive database. http://www.siap.gob.mx/resumen-nacional-pecuario/(accessed March 23, 2014).

México, Secretaría de Agricultura, Ganadería, Desarrollo Rural, Pesca, y Alimentación, Servicio Nacional de Sanidad, Inocuidad, y Calidad Agroalimentaria (SAGARPA/SENASICA), Dirección General de Salud Animal, Dirección de Epidemiologia y Análisis de Riesgo. (2014). "Situación Zoosanitaria en los Estados de la República Mexicana." November 10. http://www.senasica.gob.mx/?doc=26787 (accessed December 4, 2014).

México, Secretaría de Economía. (2012). "Resolución Final de la investigación antidumping sobre las importaciones de pierna y muslo de pollo originarias de los Estados Unidos de América, inde- pendientemente del país de procedencia. Estas mercancías se clasifican en las fracciones arancel-arias 0207.13.03 y 0207.14.04 de la Tarifa de la Ley de los Impuestos Generales de Importación y de Exportación." *Diario Oficial de la Federación*, June 8. http://dof.gob.mx/nota_detalle.php?codigo=5262441&fecha=06/08/2012 (accessed August 2013).

_______. (2011a). "Mexico y Estados Unidos Pactan Solución al Conflicto de Autotransporte Transfronterizo de Carga." Boletín de Prensa No. 40. March 3. www.economia.gob.mx/swb/es/ economia/p_noticia_0 (accessed March 4, 2011).

_______. (2011b). "Resolución por la que se acepta la solicitud de parte interesada y se declara el inicio de la investigación antidumping sobre las importaciones de pierna y muslo de pollo, originarias de los Estados Unidos de América, independientemente del país de procedencia." *Diario Oficial*. February 8. (accessed February 14, 2011).

_______. (2011c). *Tratado de Libre Comercio entre México y Costa Rica, Guatemala, Honduras y Nicaragua. Ficha Informativa*. November. http://www.economia.gob.mx/files/comunidad_nego-cios/comercio_exterior/TLC_Unico_ficha.pdf.

México, Secretaría de Economía, Dirección General de Inversión Extranjera. (2014). "Flujos totales de IED hacia México por tipo de inversión, país de origen, sector económico y entidad federa- tiva de destino (1999-2013)." Spreadsheet. http://www.economia.gob.mx/comunidad-negocios/competitividad-normatividad/inversion-extranjera-directa/estadistica-oficial-de-ied-en-mexico (accessed March 19, 2014).

México, Secretaría de Economía, Unidad de Prácticas Comerciales Internacionales (UPCI). (2014). *Estadísticas de UPCI.* http://www.economia.gob.mx/comunidad-negocios/industria-y-comercio/upci/estadisticas (accessed October 9, 2014).

Miller, Susie, & Charles Parrott. (2014). "RCC Action Plan Item: Financial Protection for Produce Sellers." U.S.-Canada Regulatory Cooperation Council (RCC) Webinar Presentation. January. http://www.trade.gov/rcc/rcc-webinar-presentations-january2014.asp (accessed May 12, 2014).

Mitchell, Diana, Rhonda Skaggs, William Gorman, Terry Crawford & Leland Southard. (2001). "Mexican Cattle Exports to U.S.: Current Perspectives." U.S. Department of Agriculture, Economic Research Service, *Agricultural Outlook* (June-July): 6-9. www.ers.usda.gov/publications/agoutlook/june2001/ao282d.pdf (accessed December 16, 2008).

Motamed, Mesbah, Kenneth A. Foster, & Wallace E. Tyner. (2008). "Applying Cointegration and Error Correction to Measure Trade Linkages: Maize Prices in the United States and Mexico." *Agricultural Economics*, *38*, 29-39.

NAFTA Secretariat. (2014). *Status Report of Panel Proceedings.* https://www.nafta-sec-alena.org/ Default.aspx?tabid=94&language=en-US (accessed October 8, 2014).

North American Free Trade Agreement Arbitral Panel Established Pursuant to Chapter Twenty in the Matter of Cross-Border Trucking Services (NAFTA Arbitral Panel). (2001). "Final Report of the Panel." Secretariat File No. USA-MEX-98-2008-01, February 6. http://registry.nafta-sec-alena.org/cmdocuments/8f70c18a-7f02-4126-96f6-182a11c90517.pdf (accessed March 9, 2011).

North American Plant Protection Organization. (2011). *Guidelines to Understanding NAPPO.* April 20. http://www.nappo.org/en/data/files/download/PDF/Introduction%20to%20NAPPO-April%202011-e.pdf (accessed October 10, 2014).

Office of the United States Trade Representative (USTR). (2011a). "Joint Statement from the January 10, 2011 Meeting of the NAFTA Free Trade Commission (FTC), in Mexico City, Mexico." Press release.

www.ustr.gov/about-us/press-office/press-releases/2011/january/joint-statement-january-10-2011-meeting-nafta-free (accessed January 13, 2011).

____. (2011b). "Trans-Pacific Partnership." February 18. www.ustr.gov/tpp (accessed March 2, 2011).

Olson, Pete. (2014). *Update: U.S. Fresh Potato Exports—Border Access Resumes*. U.S. Department of Agriculture, Foreign Agricultural Service, Global Agricultural Information Network Report No. MX4055. July 7. http://gain.fas.usda.gov/Recent%20GAIN%20Publications/UPDATE%20 U.S.%20Fresh%20Potato%20Exports%e2%80%94Border%20Access%20 Resumes_Mexico_ Mexico_7-7-2014.pdf (accessed September 16, 2014).

Olson, Pete, & Dulce Flores. (2014). *Mexico Potato Market Opens*. U.S. Department of Agriculture, Foreign Agricultural Service, Global Agricultural Information Network Report No. MX4041. May 21. http://gain.fas.usda.gov/Recent%20GAIN%20Publications/Mexican%20P otato%20Market%20Opens_Mexico_Mexico_5-21-2014.pdf (accessed June 17, 2014).

Organization of Economic Cooperation and Development (OECD). (2014). *Glossary of Statistical Terms*. http://stats.oecd.org/glossary/index.htm (accessed November 5, 2014).

Peel, Derrell S., Kenneth H. Mathews, Jr., & Rachel J. Johnson. (2011). *Trade, the Expanding Mexican Beef Industry, and Feedlot and Stocker Cattle Production in Mexico*. U.S. Department of Agriculture, Economic Research Service, Outlook Report No. LDP-M-206-01. August. http:// www.ers.usda.gov/media/118317/ldpm20601.pdf (accessed April 4, 2014).

Pequignot, Corinne, & Tim McGrath. (2014). "Mutual Reliance of Food Testing Results." U.S.- Canada Regulatory Cooperation Council Webinar. January. http://www.trade.gov/rcc/rcc-webinar-presentations-january 2014.asp.

Perez, Agnes, & Kristy Plattner. (2013). *Fruit and Tree Nuts Yearbook Tables*. U.S. Department of Agriculture, Economic Research Service. November 19. http://www.ers.usda.gov/data-products/fruit-and-tree-nut-data/ yearbook-tables.aspx (accessed April 9, 2014).

Pérez U. Matilde. (2014). "México no viola ninguna ley al exportar azúcar a EU: Sagarpa." *La Jornada* (Mexico City), April 28. http://www.jornada. unam.mx/2014/04/28/politica/022n1pol (accessed May 9, 2014).

Persaud, Suresh. (2014). *Agricultural Trade Multipliers*. Data set. U.S. Department of Agriculture, Economic Research Service, February 4.

http://www.ers.usda.gov/data-products/agricultural- trade-multipliers.aspx (accessed March 10, 2014).

Polek, MaryLou. (2014). "Industry Perspective: The Challenge of Managing Huanglongbing (HLB) and its Vector, the Asian Citrus Psyllid (ACP)." Presentation delivered at the 2014 Agricultural Outlook Forum, U.S. Department of Agriculture, Arlington, VA, February 21. http://www.usda.gov/oce/forum/friday.htm#friday10 (accessed July 17, 2014).

Rathlou, Mary, & Mary Stanley. (2014). "Equivalence of Food Safety Systems, Meat and Poultry Export Certification." U.S.-Canada Regulatory Cooperation Council Webinar. January. http://www.trade.gov/rcc/rcc-webinar-presentations-january2014.asp.

San Juan, Zaida. (2010). *Mexico Lifts Ban on Poultry Imports from Four U.S. Counties*. U.S. Department of Agriculture, Foreign Agricultural Service, Global Agricultural Information Network Report, not numbered. September 21. http://gain.fas.usda.gov/Recent%20GAIN%20Publications/Mexico%20Lifts%20Ban%20on%20Poultry%20Imports%20from%20Four%20U.S.%20Counties_Mexico_Mexico_9-21-2010.pdf (accessed March 31, 2014).

____. (2009). *Mexico Bans Poultry Imports from Two Tennessee Counties*. U.S. Department of Agriculture, Foreign Agricultural Service, Global Agricultural Information Network Report No. MX9034. May 21. http://gain.fas.usda.gov/Recent%20GAIN%20Publications/Mexico%20Bans%20Poultry%20Imports%20from%20Two%20Tennessee%20Counties%20_Mexico_ Mexico_5-21-2009.pdf (accessed December 29, 2010).

Schluter, Gerald, & Fred, Gale. (1996). "NAFTA and Employment: Has It Mattered?" Paper presented at the NAFTA Symposium organized by the Texas A&M University's Texas Agribusiness Market Research Center, October 29. http://agrinet.tamu.edu/trade/papers/ naftaemp.pdf (accessed February 20, 2007).

Schnepf, Randy. (2004). U.S.-Canada Wheat Trade Dispute. CRS Report for Congress, Order Code RL32426, Congressional Research Service, The Library of Congress, updated version, June 14. www.ncseonline.org/NLE/CRSreports/04Jun/RL32426.pdf.

Statistics Canada. (2014). "Table 002-0011 - Food available in Canada, annual (kilograms per person, per year unless otherwise noted)." *CANSIM* (database). May 30.

Statistics Canada, CATSNET Analytics. (2014). "Canadian Agri-Food Exports to Mexico 1988-2003" and "Canadian Agri-food Imports from Mexico

1988-2003." Spreadsheets obtained directly from Statistics Canada. March 21.

Stover, Ed. (2014). "Citrus Greening Research: Challenges, Success and the Future." Presentation delivered at the 2014 Agricultural Outlook Forum, U.S. Department of Agriculture, Arlington, VA, February 21. http://www.usda.gov/oce/forum/friday.htm#friday10 (accessed July 17, 2014).

Supermercados Internacionales H-E-B. (2014). "Nuestras Tiendas." Webpage. http://www. hebmexico.com/Nuestras-Tiendas/ (accessed December 4, 2014).

Taylor, Michael. (2013). "Statement from FDA Deputy Commissioner for Foods and Veterinary Medicine, Michael Taylor, on Key Provisions of the Proposed FSMA Rules Affecting Farmers." U.S. Food and Drug Administration, December. http://www.fda.gov/Food/ GuidanceRegulation/ FSMA/ucm379397.htm (accessed May 9, 2014).

The Packer. (2014). "NEW UPDATE: U.S. Revokes PACA Status for Canadian Shippers. October 2. http://www.thepacker.com/fruit-vegetable-news/US-revokes-privileged-PACA-status-for- Canadian-suppliers-277936351.html?view=all (accessed October 20, 2014).

Thornsbury, Suzanne, Hodan Farah Wells & Jennifer Bond. (2013). *Vegetables and Pulses Yearbook Tables*. U.S. Department of Agriculture, Economic Research Service. October 21. http://www.ers.usda.gov/data-products/vegetables-and-pulses-data/yearbook-tables.aspx#29677 (accessed April 3, 2014).

Ting, Kathryn. (2014). *Canada Grain and Feed Annual 2014*. U.S. Department of Agriculture, Foreign Agricultural Service, Global Agricultural Information Network Report No. CA14036. April 2. http://gain.fas.usda.gov/Recent%20GAIN%20Publications/Grain%20and %20Feed%20Annual_Ottawa_Canada_4-2-2014.pdf (accessed May 13, 2014).

U.S. Department of Agriculture, Agricultural Marketing Service (USDA/AMS). (2006-14). *Grains Inspected and/or Weighed for Export by Region and Country of Destination*. WA_GR108, various issues. http://search.ams.usda.gov/mnsearch/mnsearch.aspx.

____. (2013). "Mandatory Country of Origin Labeling of Beef, Pork, Lamb, Chicken, Goat Meat, Wild and Farm-Raised Fish and Shellfish, Perishable Agricultural Commodities, Peanuts, Pecans, Ginseng, and Macadamia Nuts." *Federal Register*, Vol. *78*, No. 101 (May 24), 31367-85.

http://www.gpo.gov/fdsys/pkg/FR-2013-05-24/pdf/2013-12366.pdf (accessed July 17, 2014).

_______. (2009). "Mandatory Country of Origin Labeling of Beef, Pork, Lamb, Chicken, Goat Meat, Wild and Farm-Raised Fish and Shellfish, Perishable Agricultural Commodities, Peanuts, Pecans, Ginseng, and Macadamia Nuts." *Federal Register*, Vol. *74*, No. 10 (January 15), 2658-2707. www.ams.usda.gov/AMSv1.0/getfile?dDocName=STELPRDC 5074925

___. (1991-2005). *Grain and Feed Weekly Summary and Statistics.* Various issues. http://search. ams.usda.gov/mnsearch/mnsearch.aspx.

U.S. Department of Agriculture, Animal and Plant Health Inspection Service (USDA/APHIS). (2014a). "Animal Disease Status: List of USDA-Recognized Animal Health Status of Countries/Regions Regarding Specific Livestock or Poultry Diseases, or Acceptable Commodities." September 2. http://www.aphis.usda.gov/wps/portal/banner/help? 1dmy& urile=wcm%3Apath%3A%2Faphis_content_library%2Fsa_our_focus%2F sa_animal_health%2Fsa_import_into_us%2Fct_animal_disease_status

___. (2014b). "Restrictions on the Importation of Fresh Pork and Pork Products from a Region in Mexico." *Federal Register*, Vol. *79*, No. 145, July 29: 43974-43980. https://www.federal- register.gov/articles/2014/ 07/29/2014-17886/restrictions-on-the-importation-of-fresh-pork-and-pork-products-from-a-region-in-mexico (accessed November 5, 2014).

___. (2006). "Bovine Spongiform Encephalopathy: An Overview," Program Aid No. 1705. www. aphis.usda.gov/publications/animal_health/ content/printable_version/BSEbrochure12-2006.pdf (accessed December 19, 2008).

U.S. Department of Agriculture, Animal and Plant Health Inspection Service (USDA/APHIS), Veterinary Services. (2012). *Summary Report California Bovine Espongiform Encephalopathy Case Investigation.* July. http://www.aphis.usda.gov/animal_health/animal_diseases/bse/down-loads/BSE_Summary_Report.pdf (accessed March 31, 2014).

U.S. Department of Agriculture, Economic Research Service (USDA/ERS). (2014a). *Food Availability (Per Capita) Data System (FADS).* Interactive database, February 1. http://www. ers.usda.gov/data-products/food-availability-(per-capita)-data-system.aspx (accessed March 24, 2014).

___. (2014b). *International Macroeconomic Data Set.* http://www.ers. usda.gov/data-products/international-macroeconomic-data-set.aspx (accessed October 10, 2014).

_______. (2013). *Raw-Fiber Equivalents of U.S. Textile Trade Data.* November 19. http://www.ers. usda.gov/data-products/cotton,-wool,-and-textile-data/raw-fiber-equivalents-of-us-textile-trade- data.aspx (accessed November 5, 2014).

U.S. Department of Agriculture, Food Safety and Inspection Service (USDA/FSIS). (2014). *Countries/Products Eligible for Export to the United States.* http://www.fsis.usda.gov/wps/wcm/ connect/4872809d-90c6-4fa6-a2a8-baa77f48e9af/Countries_Products_Eligible_ for_Export%2B. pdf?MOD=AJPERES (accessed October 8, 2014).

U.S. Department of Agriculture, Foreign Agricultural Service (USDA/FAS). (2014a). *Global Agricultural Trade System Online.* Interactive database. www.fas.usda.gov/gats.

___. (2014b). *Production, Supply and Distribution (PSD) Online.* Interactive database. www.fas. usda.gov/psdonline/psdQuery.aspx (accessed April 3, 2014).

U.S. Department of Agriculture, National Agricultural Statistics Service (USDA/NASS). (2014a). *Farm Labor.* May 22. http://usda.mannlib. cornell.edu/usda/current/FarmLabo/ FarmLabo-05-22-2014.pdf (accessed June 4, 2014).

___. (2014b). *Quick Stats 2.0.* http://quickstats.nass.usda.gov/ (accessed October 10, 2014).

___. (2013a). *Citrus Fruits: 2013 Summary.* September 19. http://usda.mannlib.cornell.edu/usda/current/CitrFrui/CitrFrui-09-23-2010_new_format.pdf (accessed March 17, 2014).

_______. (2013b). *Noncitrus Fruits and Nuts: 2012 Preliminary Summary.* January 25. http://usda01. library.cornell.edu/usda/current/NoncFruiNu/ NoncFruiNu-01-25-2013.pdf (accessed March 17,2014).

___. (2013c). *Vegetables: 2012 Summary.* January 29. http://usda.mannlib. cornell.edu/MannUsda/viewDocumentInfo.do?documentID=1183 (accessed March 17, 2014).

___. (1994a). *Noncitrus Fruits and Nuts: 1993 Summary.* July. http://usda.mannlib.cornell.edu/usda/nass/NoncFruiNu//1990s/1994/NoncFruiNu-07-00-1994.pdf (accessed January 26, 2011).

___. (1994b). *Vegetables: 1993 Summary: Reissued.* February. http://usda.mannlib.cornell.edu/usda/nass/VegeSumm//1990s/1994/VegeSumm-02-00-1994.pdf (accessed January 26, 2011).

___. (1993). *Citrus Fruits: 1993 Summary.* September. http:// usda.mannlib.cornell.edu/usda/nass/ CitrFrui//1990s/1993/CitrFrui-09-00-1993.pdf (accessed January 26, 2011).

U.S. Department of Commerce, Bureau of Economic Analysis (USDOC/BEA). 2014a. International Data: Direct Investment & Multinational Enterprises (MNEs). December 10. http://www.bea.gov/iTable/index_MNC.cfm (accessed December 10, 2014).

____. (2014b). *U.S. International Economic Accounts: Concepts and Methods.* June 30. http://www. bea.gov/international/pdf/concepts-methods/ONE%20PDF%20-%20IEA%20Concepts%20Methods.pdf (accessed September 16, 2014).

U.S. Department of Commerce, Bureau of the Census. (2013). *International Data Base*. December 19. http://www.census.gov/population/international/data/idb/informationGateway.php (accessed March 18, 2014).

U.S. Department of Commerce, International Trade Administration (USDOC/ITA). (2014a). *Fact Sheet: Commerce Preliminarily Finds Countervailable Subsidization of Imports of Sugar from Mexico*. August 26. http://enforcement.trade.gov/download/factsheets/factsheet-mexico-sugar- ad-prelim-082614.pdf (accessed September 25, 2014).

____. (2014b). "Notice: Sugar from Mexico: Postponement of Preliminary Determination of Antidumping Duty Investigation." *Federal Register*, August 21, p. 19874. https://www.federal- register.gov/articles/2014/08/21/2014-19874/sugar-from-mexico-postponement-of-preliminary-determination-of-antidumping-duty-investigation (accessed September 25, 2014).

____. (2014c). "Fact Sheet: Commerce Preliminarily Finds Dumping of Imports of Sugar from Mexico." October 27. http://enforcement.trade.gov/download/factsheets/factsheet-mexico-sugar- ad-prelim-102714.pdf (accessed November 5, 2014).

____. (2013). "Commerce Signs Antidumping Suspension Agreement on Imports of Fresh Tomatoes from Mexico." March 4. https://docs.google.com/file/d/0B5zj3ReYtLYXQmxueUI2WEdzYk0/edit?usp=sharing&pli=1 (accessed May 12, 2014).

____. (2010). "Foreign Retaliations." September 2. http://trade.gov/mas/ian/tradedisputes-enforce- ment/retaliations/tg_ian_002094.asp

U.S. Department of Commerce, Office of Textiles and Apparel. (2010). "U.S. Imports of Textiles and Apparel." Interactive database, December 16. http://otexa.ita.doc.gov/scripts/tqads2.exe/ctrypage (accessed December 16, 2010).

U.S. Department of Health and Human Services and U.S. Department of Agriculture. (2010). *Dietary Guidelines for Americans, 2010*. 7th Edition. Washington, DC: U.S. Government Printing Office. December.

http://www.health.gov/dietaryguidelines/dga2010/DietaryGuidelines2010.pdf (accessed September 13, 2014).

U.S. Department of Labor, Bureau of Labor Statistics. (1994-2014). "Household Data: Annual Averages: Table 18: Employed persons by detailed industry, sex, race, and Hispanic origin," *Employment and Earnings*, various issues, January. www.bls.gov/cps/tables.htm#annual.

U.S. Department of Labor, Employment and Training Administration, Office of Foreign Labor Certification (USDOL/ETA). (2013). "H-2A Temporary Agricultural Labor Certification Program– Selected Statistics, FY 2013." http://www.foreignlaborcert.doleta.gov/pdf/H-2A_Selected_Statistics_FY2013_YTD_Q4_final.pdf (accessed June 4, 2014).

U.S. Food and Drug Administration (FDA). (2014a). *FSMA Proposed Rule for Foreign Supplier Verification Programs (FSVP) for Importers of Food for Humans and Animals*. October 7. http://www.fda.gov/Food/GuidanceRegulation/FSMA/ucm361902.htm (accessed October 22, 2014).

____. (2014b). *FSMA Proposed Rule for Produce Safety: Standards for the Growing, Harvesting, Packing, and Holding of Produce for Human Consumption*. September 20. http://www.fda.gov/Food/GuidanceRegulation/FSMA/ucm334114.htm (accessed September 25, 2014).

____. (2013a). *FSMA Facts: Proposed Rule for Produce Safety*. http://www.fda.gov/downloads/Food/GuidanceRegulation/FSMA/UCM359258.pdf (accessed May 9, 2014).

____. (2013b). *2013 Annual Report on Food Facilities, Food Imports, and FDA Foreign Offices*. November. http://www.fda.gov/Food/GuidanceRegulation/FSMA/ucm376478.htm (accessed May 9, 2014).

____. (2010). "Memoranda of Understanding and Other Cooperative Agreements: FDA-CFIA, Canada." Webpage. http://www.fda.gov/internationalprograms/agreements/memorandaofunder-standing/ ucm 107556.htm (accessed October 20, 2014).

____. (2009). "FDA Expands Presence Outside U.S. with Opening of Mexico City Post." Webpage. December 15. www.fda.gov/InternationalPrograms/FDABeyondOurBordersForeignOffices/ LatinAmerica/ucm201034.htm (accessed March 3, 2011).

U.S. International Trade Commission (USITC). (2014a). "Antidumping and Countervailing Duty Orders in Place as of August 27, 2014." August 27. http://usitc.gov/trade_remedy/ (accessed October 9, 2014).

____. (2014b). "Sugar from Mexico; Institution of Antidumping and Countervailing Duty Investigations and Scheduling of Preliminary Phase

Investigations." *Federal Register*, Vol. 79, No. 64 (April 3), 18697-98. https://www.federalregister.gov/articles/2014/04/03/2014-07420/ sugar-from-mexico-institution-of-antidumping-and-countervailing-duty-investigations-and- scheduling (accessed April 7, 2014).

___. (2013). "Fresh Tomatoes From Mexico: Suspension of Antidumping Investigation." *Federal Register* (March 8): 14967-79. http://www.ustr.gov/about-us/press-office/reports-and-publica- tions/2013/final-report-us-eu-hlwg (accessed May 12, 2014).

___. (2009). *Modifications to the Harmonized Tariff Schedule of the United States to Adjust Rules of Origin under the North American Free Trade Agreement*. Publication 4095. August. www. usitc.gov/publications/tariff_affairs/pub4095.pdf (accessed January 4, 2011).

U.S.-Mexico High-Level Regulatory Cooperation Council (HLRCC). (2013). *U.S.-Mexico High- Level Regulatory Cooperation Council: Progress Report to Leaders*. August 15. http://www. trade.gov/hlrcc/ (accessed May 9, 2014).

Valverde, Alicia. (2014). "Industriales surtirán etanol a Pemex." *Excelsior* (Mexico City), April 29, "Dinero" section, p. 9. http://www.excelsior.com.mx/periodico/flip-dinero/29-04-2014/portada. pdf (accessed May 9, 2014).

Wal-Mart de México y Centroamérica. (2014). "Nuestros Negocios: México." Webpage. http://www. walmartmexicoycam.com/negocios_mexico_a.html (accessed December 4, 2014).

White House. (2011). "Fact Sheet: Enhancing U.S.-Mexico Cooperation." Office of the Press Secretary, Statements & Releases. March 3. www.whitehouse.gov/the-press-office/2011/03/03/ fact-sheet-enhancing-us-mexico-cooperation (accessed March 4, 2011).

Williams, Daniel R., II. (2009). *Mexico Bans Poultry Imports from a County in Minnesota*. U.S. Department of Agriculture, Foreign Agricultural Research Service, Global Agriculture Information Network Report. No. MX9062. September 10. http://gain.fas.usda.gov/Recent%20GAIN%20Publications/Mexico%20Bans%20Poultry%20Imports%20from%20a%20County%20in%20Minnesota_Mexico_Mexico_9-10-2009.pdf (accessed December 29, 2010).

World Organization for Animal Health (OIE). (2011). *World Animal Health Information Database (WAHID)*. February 12. http://web.oie.int/wahis/public.php?page=country_reports (accessed March 8, 2011).

World Trade Organization (WTO). (2014a). "Dispute DS384: United States—Certain Country of Origin Labelling Requirements." October 20.

www.wto.org/english/tratop_e/dispu_e/cases_e/ ds384_e.htm (accessed November 5, 2014).

___. (2014b). "Dispute DS386: United States—Certain Country of Origin Labelling Requirements." January 11. www.wto.org/english/tratop_e/dispu_e/cases_e/ds386_e.htm (accessed March 28, 2014).

Zahniser, Steven. (2007). *NAFTA at 13: Implementation Nears Completion*. U.S. Department of Agriculture, Economic Research Service, Outlook Report No. WRS-07-01, March. www.ers. usda.gov/publications/wrs0701/

Zahniser, Steven (ed.). (2005). *NAFTA at 11: The Growing Integration of North American Agriculture*. U.S. Department of Agriculture, Economic Research Service, Outlook Report No. WRS-05-02, February.www.ers. usda.gov/Publications/WRS0502/wrs0502.pdf

Zahniser, Steven, & Mary Burfisher. (2007). "NAFTA at the Crossroads: Should Mexico Adopt Full Implementation in 2008?" January 29 revision. Paper presented at the 2006 Winter Meetings of the International Agricultural Trade Research Consortium (IATRC), St. Petersburg, Florida, December 3-6, 2006.

Zahniser, Steven, & Zachary Crago. (2009). *NAFTA at 15: Building on Free Trade*. U.S. Department of Agriculture, Economic Research Service, Outlook Report No. WRS-09-03, March. www.ers.usda.gov/ publications/wrs0903/

Zahniser, Steven, & Adriana Herrera Moreno. (2014). "North American Agricultural Trade Policy: Are Super-Regionalism and Deeper Regional Integration the 'Next Big Thing' after NAFTA?" *Estey Centre Journal of International Law and Trade Policy*, *15*(2), 199-231. November.

Zahniser, Steven, Tom Hertz, Peter Dixon, & Maureen Rimmer. (2012). *The Potential Impact of Changes in Immigration Policy on U.S. Agriculture and the Market for Hired Farm Labor: A Simulation Analysis*. U.S. Department of Agriculture, Economic Research Service, Economic Research Report No. 135. May. http://www.ers.usda.gov/publications/err-economic-research- report/err135.aspx (accessed October 3, 2014).

Zahniser, Steven, & John Link (eds.). (2002). *Effects of the North American Free Trade Agreement on Agriculture and the Rural Economy*. U.S. Department of Agriculture, Economic Research Service, Agriculture and Trade Report No. WRS-02-1, July. www.ers.usda.gov/publications/wrs0201/

Zahniser, Steven, Karl Meilke, & James Rude. (2009). "What's Next for NAFTA?" U.S. Department of Agriculture, Economic Research Service,

Amber Waves, Vol. 7, Issue 1 (March):2. www.ers.usda.gov/AmberWaves/March09/Findings/NAFTA.htm

Zahniser, Steven & Andrew, Roe. (2011). *NAFTA at 17: Full Implementation Leads to Increased Trade and Integration.* U.S. Department of Agriculture, Economic Research Service, Outlook Report No. WRS-11-01. March. http://www.ers.usda.gov/media/129506/wrs1101.pdf (accessed October 10, 2014).

Zahniser, Steven, Marcela Vera Torres, José Alberto Cuéllar Álvarez, Nicolás Fernando López López, & Rhea Bhatta. (2010). *The U.S. and Mexican Dry Bean Sectors.* U.S. Department of Agriculture, Economic Research Service, Outlook Report No. VGS-341-10, December, www. ers.usda.gov/Publications/VGS/2010/10Oct/VGS34101/vgs34101.pdf

End Notes

[1] We tend to use the word "NAFTA" to refer to the entire agreement, including provisions incorporated from CUSTA.

[2] The U.S. Department of Commerce, Bureau of Economic Analysis (2014b) defines FDI as the "ownership or control, directly or indirectly, by one foreign resident, the foreign parent, of at least 10 percent of a [domestic] business enterprise."

[3] The OECD (2014) defines vertical integration as "the ownership or control by a firm of different stages of the production process," while a horizontally integrated enterprise is "one in which several different kinds of activities that produce different kinds of goods or services for sale on the market are carried out in parallel with each other."

[4] Previous editions of ERS's NAFTA report are available in the NAFTA, Canada, and Mexico pages of the ERS website (http://www.ers.usda.gov/topics/international-markets-tradexico.aspx). Unlike the previous editions, this report is not prepared in response to a congressional mandate; the mandate behind the reports issued from 1995 to 2011 ended with the 2011 edition.

[5] A TRQ is a quota for a volume of imports at a generally low tariff. After the quantitative limit is reached, a higher tariff is applied on additional imports.

[6] Recently, the Canadian Government has shown some flexibility in this regard. As part of the agreement-in-principle for the Comprehensive Economic and Trade Agreement (CETA) between Canada and the European Union (EU), unveiled in October 2013, the EU secured additional duty-free access to the Canadian cheese market in the amount of 16,000 metric tons of specialty cheeses and 1,700 metric tons of industrial cheese per year, along with an additional 800 metric tons of Canada's World Trade Organization TRQ for cheese that is being reallocated to the EU in response to the EU's expansion (Government of Canada, 2013). The sum of these quantities (18,500 metric tons) corresponds to about 4 percent of Canada's domestic cheese consumption in 2013 [calculated using consumption data from Canada Dairy Information Centre (2013) and population data from U.S. Department of Commerce, Bureau of the Census (2013)].

[7] While NAFTA's transition to intraregional free trade in agricultural products ended in 2008, at least one nonagricultural product has a transitional period longer than 14 years. In 2009, Mexico started to allow the importation of used cars from the United States, and this trade will not be free of tariff restrictions until 2018.

[8] Other analytical approaches could be developed and implemented with further effort. For instance, one could use trade-to-output ratios to measure levels of economic openness or econometric methods to study the integration of com- modity prices in the NAFTA countries.

[9] The trade data in this report are drawn mainly from three sources. The *Global Agricultural Trade System (GATS)*— produced by the U.S. Department of Agriculture, Foreign Agricultural Service (2014a) using data from the U.S. Census Bureau—is the primary source of the U.S. agricultural trade data, including data on bilateral trade between the United States and its NAFTA partners. The GATS data are routinely updated, so the values in this report may not precisely match the most recent values in GATS. When the GATS data are not sufficient, trade statistics published by the Canadian and Mexican Governments are used. Statistics Canada, CATSNET Analytics (2014) is the source of the Canadian statistics, while Mexico's Secretaría de Economía—as cited by Global Trade Information Services (2014)—is the source of the Mexican statistics. Unless otherwise indicated, trade values are in nominal terms.

[10] When one subtracts Canada-Mexico agricultural trade from intraregional agricultural trade, one gets the value of U.S. agricultural trade with Canada and Mexico. In 2013, U.S. agricultural trade with its NAFTA partners equaled $78.9 billion, compared with $16.3 billion in 1993 and $8.5 billion in 1989.

[11] Sorghum exports to Canada are not listed in figure 2 because Canada uses limited amounts of sorghum in its feed rations and imports only small quantities of that commodity. By contrast, Mexico is the leading importer of U.S. sorghum, accounting for 64 percent of total U.S. sorghum exports during 2011-13. U.S. sorghum exports to Mexico averaged 1.5 million metric tons per year during this period, compared with roughly 3,000 metric tons to Canada.

[12] Protected agriculture is a term that refers to a variety of productive techniques, including greenhouses, row covers, drip irrigation, temperature controls, and the use of mulch.

[13] As with all trade multipliers, care must be taken in the interpretation of the resulting estimate because it does not account for price changes or structural changes in the economy since 2002, the year for which the benchmark table was constructed. The ERS Agricultural Trade Multipliers (Persaud, 2014) enable users to work with predefined multipliers and to create their own multipliers.

[14] One must be cautious when comparing production data across long time periods, as unusual weather patterns may make the selected time periods in the comparison to be unrepresentative. For instance, lower yields for tart cherries and grapes during 2010-12 were linked to adverse weather conditions in one or more of those years. In addition, the emergence in the United States of the citrus disease called citrus greening, also known as Huanglongbing (HLB), has adversely affected U.S. orange production. USDA's 2014 Agricultural Outlook Forum devoted an entire session to this subject. For more information on the presentations by this panel, see Hebbar (2014), Polek (2014), and Stover (2014).

[15] Appendix table 5 provides a more detailed breakdown of U.S., Canadian, and Mexican direct investment in the North American processed food sector.

[16] The years 1989-92 are used as the pre-NAFTA period for purposes of comparison because U.S. corn exports to Mexico were unusually low in 1993, the last year prior to NAFTA's implementation.

[17] Per capita consumption levels were calculated using consumption estimates from USDA/FAS (2014b) and population estimates from U.S. Department of Commerce, Bureau of the Census (2013).

[18] By comparison, Canada's population increased from 29 million to 35 million (19 percent) between 1993 and 2010, while the U.S. population grew from 260 million to 316 million (19 percent).

[19] We discuss exports for 2012 rather than 2013 because exports in 2013 were unusually small due to the drought of 2012.

[20] Data in this sentence were calculated using trade data from USDA/FAS (2014a) and production estimates from USDA/FAS (2014b) that correspond to marketing years rather than calendar years.

[21] See Hahn et al. (2005) for a discussion of these quotas.

[22] Responsibility for determining whether to approve the importation of meat, poultry, and egg products into the United States is shared by two USDA agencies. USDA's Animal and Plant Health Inspection Service (APHIS) is responsible for evaluating the animal health status of foreign countries and specific regions within those countries, as well as the risk of introducing disease into the United States via the importation of commodities from those countries or regions; these evalu- ations help to determine whether a specific country or region is eligible to export specific meat, poultry, or egg products to the United States. USDA's Food Safety and Inspection Service (FSIS) is responsible for ensuring that meat, poultry, and egg products imported to the United States are produced under standards equivalent to U.S. inspection standards and are safe, wholesome, unadulterated, and properly labeled and packaged. In the countries that are eligible to export such products to the United States, FSIS certifies and decertifies establishments that are allowed to participate in this trade, and it audits the inspection systems of those countries. USDA/APHIS (2014a) summarizes the evaluations of the animal health status of foreign countries with respect to certain diseases, while USDA/FSIS (2014) contains the audit reports and lists of foreign establishments.

[23] Mexican tariffs on U.S. and Canadian beef offals, however, were phased out over a 9-year period.

[24] BSE is a fatal neurological disease in adult cattle that is also a concern to human health. Some studies have linked the agent that causes BSE to a similar disorder in humans, most likely through the consumption of food ingredients obtained from BSE-infected cattle (USDA/APHIS, 2006).

[25] A total of 17 animals in Canada have been discovered to have BSE since May 2003. The most recent Canadian discovery (February 2010) was a 71-month-old beef cow in Alberta (Canadian Food Inspection Agency, 2014). In the United States, a total of 4 animals have been discovered to have BSE since May 2003. The most recent U.S. discovery (April 2012) was a dairy cow at the age of 10 years and 7 months in California (USDA/APHIS, Veterinary Services, 2012). No BSE discoveries have been reported for Mexico.

[26] Detailed summaries of these efforts are available in Zahniser and Crago (2009) and Zahniser (2007).

[27] The trade data in this section include fruit and vegetable juice as part of the total trade in fruit and vegetables.

[28] The statistics in this paragraph were calculated using U.S. per capita food availability data from USDA/ERS (2014), and import data from U.S. Department of Commerce, Bureau of the Census, *Foreign Trade Statistics*, as cited by USDA/ FAS (2014a).

[29] Dry beans are classified as a vegetable in USDA's *Foreign Agricultural Trade of the United States* data system and as both a vegetable and a protein food in the *Dietary Guidelines for Americans* (U.S. Department of Health and Human Services and U.S. Department of Agriculture, 2010). Yet the U.S. dry bean sector resembles the U.S. grain and oilseeds sector in terms of large farms and capital intensity—both features that reflect the comparative advantage of U.S. dry bean exporters—and many U.S. dry bean farmers also grow grains and/or oilseeds.

[30] An ERS report co-authored with investigators from SAGARPA (Zahniser et al., 2010) provides a fuller analysis of the U.S. and Mexican dry bean sectors.

[31] The FDA is the Federal agency responsible for the safety of all food products, with some exceptions, including meat, poultry, and egg products, which are primarily regulated by USDA's Food Safety and Inspection Service (FSIS).

[32] In 2012, Canada enacted a major food safety law of its own, called the Safe Food for Canadians Act.

[33] The figures cited in this sentence are approximate and may be revised as the records for FY 2012 are finalized.

[34] The figure of 12 percent is calculated using the import and total supply data from Haley (2014a).

[35] The per capita consumption statistics were calculated using population estimates from U.S. Department of Commerce, Bureau of the Census (2013), U.S. HFCS consumption estimates from Haley (2013), and Mexican HFCS consumption estimates from Haley (2014c).

[36] Costa Rica, the other member country of CAFTA-DR, was the 23rd leading destination of U.S. cotton textile exports in 2013.

[37] Some portions of the next two sections are drawn from Zahniser and Herrera Moreno (2014).

[38] A customs union is a free-trade area in which the member countries share a set of common external tariffs (CETs), while a common market is a customs union with the additional features of free movement of labor and capital.

[39] See U.S. Department of Commerce, Bureau of the Census (2013) for a list of the countries defined as part of the Near East.

INDEX

#

A

B

C

D

E

F

N

O

P

Q

R

S

T

U

V

W

Y